FOR EVERYBODY WHO HAS EVER FELT DAUNTED BY THE SIZE AND CO... ...RE • GOD HAS PLANS FOR A COMMUNITY AND THE COVENANT IS HIS PROMISE TO THEM

SIGNED · SEALED
DELIVERED

Text copyright © Michael Saward 2004
Illustrations copyright © Jane Bottomley 2004
The author asserts the moral right
to be identified as the author of this work

Published by
The Bible Reading Fellowship
First Floor, Elsfield Hall
15–17 Elsfield Way, Oxford OX2 8FG

ISBN 1 84101 248 3
First published 2004
10 9 8 7 6 5 4 3 2 1 0
All rights reserved

Printed and bound in Great Britain by
Bookmarque, Croydon

FOR EVERYBODY WHO HAS EVER FELT DAUNTED BY THE SIZE AND COMPLEXITY OF THE BIBLE • GOD HAS PLANS FOR A COMMUNITY AND THE COVENANT IS HIS PROMISE TO THEM

SIGNED · SEALED DELIVERED

Finding the key to the Bible

Michael Saward

For
Bob and Lynne Libby
Friends for half a lifetime and companions
in the journey of God's people of the promise

I much appreciate the advice, encouragement and
constructive criticism that I have received from
Naomi Starkey, Eithne Nutt, Karen Laister,
Lisa Cherrett, Louise Belcher and Jane Bottomley
in preparing and publishing this book.

CONTENTS

1 Clearing the Ground 6

2 Planting the Tree 9

3 Branching Out...25

4 The Tree of Life 57

5 Bearing Fruit...89

6 A Promise Fulfilled..95

   Notes 117

CLEARING THE GROUND

So what are we to make of this amazing book? Until recent years it looked forbidding, with its black cover and its gilded page-ends. What was worse was the awful memory of being a teenager at school, sub-merged in a mass of ancient dates, pages of 'so-and-so begat so-and-so' (so what?) and characters with tortu-ous and unpronounceable multi-syllabic names like Maher-shalal-hash-baz and Tiglath-pileser (who he?). Hundreds of them, it seemed, and more than enough to turn off any sensible reader for life.

Not only that, but they seemed to spend much of their time marching around from one bit of parched desert to another, from Taberah via Kibroth-hattaavah to Hazeroth and then on to Iye-abarim and the Wadi Zered, indulging in punch-ups with locals like King Og (whose tribe they cheerfully killed off) and telling each other about the famous talking donkey on the road to Kiriath-huzoth.

Had enough yet? I certainly had when I first came across this dreary and bloodthirsty lot in the early part of that black-covered leatherbound book some 60 years ago.

It was, believe it or not, the Holy Book—'Book', that is, being the English word for the ancient Greek word *biblos*. Funny thing, that. A book and yet, apparently, a whole library of scrolls, letters, poems and so on, 66 of them in all. Funny, too, that this mixed bag of wars, murders, adulteries, laws about menstruation, butchery of animals, emission of semen, and witchcraft—yes, surprise, surprise, the whole lot within those black leather covers—is called 'holy'.

The 'Holy Bible'. So you want to know about God and spirituality, and, lo and behold, he's all wrapped up in this weird barrel of garbage!

So, I ask again, what on earth are we to make of this extraordinary book? And if there really is a core of vital spirituality somewhere in it, why, oh why, is it submerged in this confusing jumble of material?

Realistically, there's not much point in asking that final question. Whether we like it or not, that's what it is. In fairness, we might as well recognize that the book, because it is a massive library, has come down to us from many hands and was composed (or perhaps edited) over the space of a thousand years from a mixture of oral traditions, written histories, poems, prophecies, gospels, letters and so on. It incorporates material in Aramaic, Hebrew and Greek and reached us after many centuries of Latin dominance, even though that element is much less influential than it would have been 500 years ago.

If, then, we're going to make real sense of it, we have to ask one or two crucial questions, not only about the content and style of the many and disparate parts of the book and how we are to set about interpreting it, but also, perhaps even more fundamentally, whether it is just a ragbag of ideas or whether there is anything that gives it some kind of coherent shape.

It's that final question that this book is going to attempt to answer. It's time to look at it more carefully.

PLANTING THE TREE

As we've already recognized, the Bible is a huge and complex book (and we'll call it that even if it is a library) which is desperately daunting to the ordinary person who opens it with the very natural assumption that it will begin at the beginning and work its way logically from there to the end. After all, that is the usual way that books are written.

Well, it isn't as simple as that. True, it all starts with the words 'in the beginning' and winds up 1164 pages later (or thereabouts) with the final word 'Amen'. So far, so good. But it doesn't simply follow a consistent time-line. The wretched thing hops about, sometimes going forward for a hundred years or more, and then, for no obvious reason, turning backwards. You could be forgiven for thinking it was a literary version of snakes and ladders, and down the ages there must have been countless people who gave up on it in disgust, never quite sure where they were and what on earth it was all about. So, we must ask, 'What is the key to the Bible?'

THE CHRONIC PROBLEM

One not altogether surprising way of handling this question has been to search for 'verses that ring a bell'.

Vast numbers of people who have wanted the Bible to speak to them as the voice of God have treated it in this way, and this method has usually gone hand in hand with a daily pattern of Bible reading. Various schemes have been published, especially in the 20th century, which set out a sequence of passages of perhaps 20 or 30 verses to be read at a time, with some helpful notes of explanation. The great temptation for the reader is to try to find a verse each day that he or she can hang on to as a 'thought for the day'.

To take an example, suppose the scheme invites the reader to turn to one of Paul's letters—say, Ephesians. Originally, of course, as with most letters, there were no 'chapters' or 'verses'. Now, for our convenience, it has become traditional, for easy reference, to refer to the letter as having six chapters, breaking up the text into 155 verses. Most modern versions of the Bible place these verses in something like 24 paragraphs. It makes sense for the reader to be offered, say, 14 sections spread over two weeks.

So, the average reader, with perhaps 15 minutes a day available, will be tempted to look each day for a 'golden verse'. It could be that on day one we choose 'God chose us… to be holy and blameless' (Ephesians 1:4). Next day it might be 'you may know what is the hope to which he has called you' (1:18). Day three produces 'by grace you have been saved' (2:5). The following day it could be 'Christ is our peace' (2:14) and day five 'you may not lose heart' (3:13). So it goes on for the full two weeks. Each day some significant (and by no means unimportant) phrase 'rings a bell'.

But there is a problem. At the end of the two weeks, our reader will have collected and enjoyed, or been challenged by, 14 phrases. But suppose the apostle Paul were to turn up at the house and say, 'What did you make of my letter, Mr Ephesian?' How would he react if our well-meaning reader said, 'Well, Paul, I'm not quite sure what it was all about but the "yours sincerely" bit was a great blessing to my soul.'

That's the problem with the 'golden verse' way of looking at the Bible. You can read it conscientiously for half a lifetime and end up with no real idea what it was all about. True, you will have been influenced by all manner of bits and pieces, but, like Little Jack Horner, you will most probably, day by day for 30 years, have simply 'put in a thumb and pulled out a plum and said "What a good boy am I"'.

You will have missed the wood for the trees. The big picture will have passed you by, so you won't really have discovered what the Bible is all about. Now, lest you think this is all unfair, let me say that over nearly half a century of ministry, I have regularly asked people who have, to my certain knowledge, regularly read the Bible on a daily basis, 'What are you reading at present?' When they tell me which book, or letter, or whatever they have been reading, and I ask them, 'What's that book (or letter, or whatever) all about?' they hardly ever know and certainly can't summarize it for me. In other words, they aren't at all clear about what the Bible is trying to say. They merely know lots of snippets, which are generally quite unconnected to each other. These readers most certainly doesn't recognize that there are major coherent ideas that integrate the Bible's meaning and transform our understanding once we have grasped them.

I suggest that we need a series of pictures to help us in this. First, we'll use the outline of a forest tree to symbolize the whole Bible, which comes out of the living nature and character of God. You can see what I mean on page 13 opposite.

Now we'll go on to look at another example of a widespread misunderstanding. As we have seen, there are 66 'books' within the Bible. The first 39 have come to be known as 'The Old Testament' and the subsequent 27 as 'The New Testament'. Many Christian people assume, therefore, that there is a distinct contrast between 'the front of the book' (the so-called Old Testament) and 'the back of the book' (what we call the New Testament). For too many people, these two parts are assumed to be in conflict. Thus, it is all too easy to fall into the trap of regarding the 'front of the book' as more or less disposable.

In the early days of the Christian Church, a wealthy ship-owner named Marcion, from Sinope, the most northern town on the Turkish coast of the Black Sea, arrived in Rome. He was rapidly thrown out of the church, and so he started creating his own churches, where he largely repudiated the Old Testament and the Jewish elements in the New Testament. To him, the God revealed in the Old Testament was an inferior being and certainly not the God and Father of Jesus. Countless people in our era, who have never heard of Marcion, share his view that Christians should reject God as found in the 'front of the book', and set 'law' and

GOD

'grace' in opposition, as well as 'flesh' and 'spirit'. Even if many present-day Christians don't go as far as that, there is a significant number who do polarize the Old and New Testaments.

The word 'testament' is, of course, rarely used in modern Bible translations. In its place is 'covenant', which more accurately reflects both the Hebrew and Greek words that were originally used (*berith* and *diatheke*). In contemporary usage, 'testament' is almost always linked with the making of a will, which has quite a different connotation from the word's meaning in the Bible.

Hebrews 8:13 uses the word 'obsolete' to describe the 'old covenant'. Thus a great many people assume that the 'front of the book'—the 'Old Testament'—is obsolete. What they fail to grasp, though, is the fact that the 'old covenant' in Hebrews is certainly not the same as the 'front of the book'. It is clearly vital that we look at what that word 'covenant' means.

THE CRUCIAL PROMISE

It is no exaggeration to say that 'covenant' is probably the most significant and important word and idea in the whole Bible. It is virtually certain that those who fail to grasp this fact and its consequences will inevitably get their overall understanding of the Bible wrong. Even words such as 'salvation', 'redemption' and 'incarnation', important though they undoubtedly are, need to be perceived as aspects of the meaning of covenant.

This, incidentally, is in no way a new idea. J.I. Packer, nearly 50 years ago, wrote in an article in *Churchman* magazine that the 'covenant' is 'the presupposition... of everything that is taught from Genesis to Revelation concerning redemption and religion, church and sacraments, and the meaning and goal of history. It integrates these doctrines into a single unified structure... it is thus the key to Biblical theology'. He concluded by declaring that 'the Bible knows no other basis for religion than God's covenant'.[1]

In the 1960s, Colin Craston, Chairman of the Anglican Consultative Council, made a very similar point. 'There is,' he wrote, 'one theme which runs right through the Bible. It is its main message... it binds all the books together. What is it? It is God's covenant.' He went on to summarize the idea by adding, 'There is one covenant of grace, planned in eternity, and worked out in this world in history'.[2]

Now we have to recognize that the Bible does not speak of only one covenant. The Old Testament introduces us to a series of covenants, and we must briefly look at these before we consider the one that is the supreme instance. First, we need to define the word itself. What is a covenant?

The one essential idea lying right at the heart of every covenant is that of promise. Covenants in the Bible are divine promises, commitments to a course of action, that God offers to his people. For a covenant to achieve its purpose, there must therefore be an agreement. God takes an initiative by making a promise that he intends to fulfil, subject always to the recipient's being ready and willing to respond to the promise. This agreement is given an accompanying sign as a permanent reminder that the agreement has been 'signed, sealed, and delivered'. Needless to say, the promise is to be beneficial to the recipient(s) who, if they are in their right mind, will always be conscious of the good thing or things that will come to them, or even through them to others.

The very earliest mention of a covenant in the Bible is made by God to the patriarch Noah. Warning Noah that all humanity had corrupted the earth with its violence and that he proposed to destroy it with a massive flood, God told Noah to build a boat (probably made of reeds) of three decks, with dimensions of 150 metres in length, 25 metres in width, and 15 metres in height. God's purpose was to provide for the continuity of every species, including humanity. The first covenant promise was that of reassurance for Noah that he and his immediate family would survive the coming cataclysm.

A consequential covenant was made when the flood subsided. On that occasion, the promise (Genesis 9:8–17) was that never again would there be a universal flood. The rainbow would be a visible sign of this promise. When rain-clouds appeared, the rainbow would be the assurance that the promise still held good and that it would apply to all living creatures.

The Old Testament has many references to covenants made by God. He made a covenant with the Jewish nation at Mount Sinai following the exodus from Egypt, and on that occasion the sign is blood, splashed over the people (Exodus 24:8). Soon after, the people betrayed him by setting up a golden calf and worshipping it. Moses, in burning anger, smashed the stone tablets containing the divine law that he had brought down from the mountain. Later, God reiterated his covenant and repeated the law on a second set of tablets (Deuteronomy 5:1–21). This covenant with the nation contained a whole series of laws (including the Ten Commandments), full provision for a system of daily and seasonal sacrifices within a holy tent, administered by a body of priests, and a range of dietary, hygienic and moral codes of practice. It was to form the basis of a complete structure of religious observance to be perennially observed by the Jewish people. Much (though by no means all) of it remains at the heart of contemporary Judaism to this day.

A later covenant, made some hundreds of years afterwards, concerned the nature and permanence of the Jewish monarchy. This promise to David (2 Samuel 23:5) was spelt out by his son, Solomon (1 Kings 8:25), in terms of a divine assurance that there would always be a successor to David on the throne of Israel. Twice in the Old Testament salt is mentioned as the sign associated with this covenant, since among Eastern people it was apparently used as a symbol of constancy and fidelity (Numbers 18:19; 2 Chronicles 13:5).

Further reminders of the significance of the covenant concept are to be found in Isaiah, Jeremiah and Ezekiel. A unique feature of the two references in Jeremiah 31:31–33 is the mention of a new covenant, which is contrasted with the Mount Sinai covenant given to the Jewish nation. It will no longer be marked by external law-keeping but will be an inner promise impacting upon the very hearts of the people. This, as we shall discover in due course, is seen to be the nature of 'the new covenant in my blood' declared by Jesus of Nazareth at the last supper (Luke 22:20). Its repercussions are eventually explained in the letter to the Hebrews (8:6–13).

None of the covenant promises so far mentioned is unimportant or insignificant. Nevertheless, only three of those in the Old Testament have the distinctive feature of being described as 'eternal' or 'everlasting'. The promise to Noah is a promise to all humanity that there will 'never again' be a universal flood. Having announced that, the matter is hardly mentioned again in the Bible.

The second of the 'eternal' covenants is that made with Abraham (and reiterated to his descendants, Isaac and Jacob). We shall return to that shortly.

Last of the three, as we have already seen, is a promise to David that his throne will never lack a successor. There is, however, a clear-cut condition attached to this promise. It will apply only if 'your children look to their way, to walk before me as you have walked before me' (1 Kings 8:25). History illustrates that time and again David's descendants fell far short of this requirement and, for all practical purposes, the monarchy died out at the time of the exile to Babylon. The Romans appointed Herod the Great as 'king of the Jews' in or about 40BC, but he was not of Jewish blood and was never really recognized by the Jewish people as their king (other than out of political necessity and the need to survive his ruthless rule).

THE CONVENIENT PICTURE

So, we turn to the 'eternal covenant' made by God with Abraham. At once we are faced with the most important of all the covenant promises and we must consider it with great care. This is the crucial promise, and all that follows in the Bible, Old and New Testaments alike, is the story and explanation of how that promise was fulfilled.

The story begins with a man whom today we would call an Iraqi setting out with his father, his wife and his nephew from a town called Ur of the Chaldees, near present-day Nasiriyah on the River Euphrates. His name was Abram, his father was Terah, his wife Sarai, and his nephew Lot. Their goal was the region of Canaan, on the western coast of Palestine, but they paused for some time in the town of Haran, close to the border between present-day Syria and Turkey. There Terah died. According to the book of Joshua (24:2), they were pagans, and it has been suggested that they worshipped the moon-god.

For our purposes, the first crucial act of the Bible's record of the patriarchal era (somewhere between 1900 and 1700BC) is the statement in Genesis (12:1–3) that God called Abram to leave Haran and travel on to Canaan. The key phrase was the covenant promise, 'I will make of you a great nation, and I will bless you, and make your name great, so that you will be a blessing… and in you all the families of the earth shall be blessed'. Abram, it is then said, 'went, as the Lord had told him' (12:4). He stopped briefly at Shechem, in the Samaritan hill country 30 miles north of Jerusalem, where an additional clause was added to the promise, namely, 'To your offspring I will give this land' (12:7). Already a man of 75, Abram had no children, his wife being 'barren' (Genesis 11:30).

Stage by stage, the covenant promise is revealed over a quarter of a century. In Genesis 13:14–17, he is assured that his descendants will be 'like the dust of the earth', in other words uncountable. By Genesis 15:5–6 a second, comparable picture, that of 'the stars in the sky', has been mentioned. Importantly, we are told that Abram 'believed the Lord; and the Lord reckoned it to him as righteousness'. On the same day, the word 'covenant' is first introduced (15:18) to describe the series of promises. This time it refers to the land to be given to Abram's descendants, ranging from the River Euphrates to the 'River of Egypt' (which commentators reckon to be the Wadi-el-Arish, south of Gaza, and not the Nile).

At last we come to the full version of the covenant, described three times in Genesis 17 as 'eternal' or 'everlasting' (vv. 7, 13, 19). Abram, now 99 years old, is reassured that the promise will indeed be to his numerous offspring, 'a multitude of nations', including kings, and God will be their God. The territorial aspect is again endorsed as 'a perpetual holding' (17:8). Two interesting new features appear. One concerns names and the other the sign and seal of the promise.

As to names, God announces that he is 'El Shaddai' (usually translated as 'God Almighty') and that from now on Abram is to bear the new name Abraham, 'the father of many nations' (17:1, 5).

The sign by which the covenant will be constantly recalled is that of circumcision. Abraham and every male in his household from then onwards is to bear the mark on his penis. Thus the males, on their bodies, and the women, in their lives, will daily be aware of the significance of the mark. 'My covenant,' says El Shaddai, 'shall be in your flesh an everlasting covenant' (17:13). Abraham circumcises Ishmael, his son by Hagar, Sarai's Egyptian slave girl, but, says David Van Biema, God 'stipulates that the covenant will flow only through Isaac's line'[3]—and as yet there is no Isaac!

God reassures Abraham and his wife (now to be called Sarah) that a son will be born to them. As Abraham will be the father of many nations, so Sarah will 'give rise to nations' (17:16) and she too will have kings from the descendants of her body. The son yet to be conceived from their elderly bodies will be called Isaac. Sarah, past the menopause, laughs at the very idea, but one year later the impossible happens. Abraham, having been circumcised along with all the males of his household to sign the acceptance of the eternal covenant promise, duly circumcises Isaac. The covenant is secured. The promise of God that in Abraham's line 'all the nations of the earth shall be blessed' has begun its long journey.

One terrible test for Abraham remains to be faced. Though he had evidently believed in the promise (15:6), he still laughed at the idea that he and Sarah would have a son. Thus, while the boy is still a child, Abraham is told to take him to a distant mountain and offer him as a sacrifice. The very thought of such a

21

demand is horrific to contemplate. Distant relatives of Abraham, however, the Ammonites, offered children to their god Molech as burnt sacrifices, so it may be that however appalling the thought would have been to Abraham, it was not a totally unknown practice. Isaac is to be sacrificed on an altar on a hill in Moriah. Later, the place is identified as the site of Solomon's temple in Jerusalem (2 Chronicles 3:1). The connection between the intended sacrifice of Isaac and the central place of sacrifice in latter-day Jerusalem (as indeed of the crucifixion of Jesus) is striking, especially to Christians.

Abraham, confident that somehow God will keep his promise, nevertheless comes to the very point of sacrificing Isaac when he is commanded to stop and, instead, to sacrifice a ram trapped nearby. The test completed, Abraham is given the repeated assurance that, having demonstrated his unconditional obedience to God, the full promise stands.

From then onwards, the Jewish people, their kings and their prophets, were all deeply conscious that they were the descendants of Abraham, Isaac and his son Jacob, and that they were inheritors of a unique covenant promise. Thus it can be fairly said (in the words of Geza Vermes) that 'the key to any understanding of Judaism must be the notion of the covenant'.[4]

And that's not all. If this 'eternal covenant' is truly 'eternal', then time has not changed it. As J.I. Packer reminds us, Abraham and his son Isaac 'became the foundation members of a community which has continued from that day to this without a break'. That community, he explains, is 'the fellowship which professes to embrace and live under God's covenant', since 'God's covenant is substantially the same today as when it was first revealed to Abraham'.[5]

In short, the Bible and history are the explanations and illustrations of how that promise was maintained by God despite the constant failures and betrayals of those within the covenant community.

If, then, you want to know how to get inside the essential meaning of the Bible, you have to start with a promise, a response and a community. What you don't do is to look for bits and pieces of private and personal so-called 'spiritual experience' on which to build a range of disconnected verses, phrases and prejudices which allow you to be 'religious'.

In other words, you have to come face to face with a God who has plans for the whole world and a people whom he has called into being to be obedient to those intentions.

It's time for our second look at that symbolic tree (overleaf). As you can see, coming out of the character of God we now have the great trunk from which all else derives. It's that covenant made by God with Abraham.

COVENANT

GOD

BRANCHING OUT

Our symbolic tree, which comes out of the very nature of God and takes as its great trunk the covenant promise made to Abraham and his descendants—that in them the whole world will be blessed—has three significant branches. These three branches lie at the very heart of the Bible, both Old and New Testaments, and virtually everything of any major importance is derived from them as twigs and leaves are connected to a tree and its branches. Thus, when we say that the covenant is the key to biblical understanding, what we mean is that wherever you open the Bible, the passage that lies before you is in some way linked to that great promise through one of the three branches. This is just as true of the history, the poetry, the letters and the Gospel narratives as it is of the vivid and colourful expectations in books like Revelation, which are called 'apocalyptic'.

At once we face a totally new situation. Instead of looking for 'golden verses' that 'ring bells', we are suddenly aware that, despite all the differences in style and the vast multiplicity of individual verses and widely varied authors coming from a range of centuries and cultures, something like a great jigsaw begins, piece by piece, to fall into place. At last we start to see how all the ideas cohere, even when at times they look to be contradicting each other and causing us, as the readers, confusion.

For a moment or two, let us change the metaphor. Suppose I am a Martian stepping out of my spacecraft on to the earth's surface. The very first thing I need, in order to make sense of where I am on this great globe, is an atlas. Once I know where I have landed and how it relates to the vastness of the planet, I can eventually ask to see an Ordnance Survey map of the immediate district. That magnificent and highly detailed chart, full of streets, houses, railways, shops and so on, will soon make real sense when I can locate what I see around me into the broader context of the world as a whole.

So it is with the Bible. Until I can see this verse, this paragraph, this story, in its correct place within the greater whole, I shall never be able to grasp what it is all about. Instead, I shall be tempted to rely on the dangerous folly of assuming that my wild guesses as to the meaning can be transformed into 'Well, I believe that the Holy Spirit is telling me it means…'. This is an extraordinarily presumptuous elevation of my ignorance into an absolute certainty that I have got God safely tucked into my pocket.

Why, then, do some people make such staggering claims of having a personal hotline to God who gives them detailed knowledge of the truth (when they hardly know one end of the Bible from the other)? The answer to that is usually rooted in a single verse in John's Gospel. On the night before his crucifixion, Jesus told his twelve disciples that the Holy Spirit, whom he would send to them, 'will guide you into all the truth'

(John 16:13). Down through the centuries, the Christian Church has understood that the reliable core of the ideas that make up the gospel are 'apostolic' in character. To those disciples, who became the apostles (which means the 'sent-out' ones), the essential truth will be conveyed by the Spirit, who will help them to recall and understand what Jesus said and did, and how this fulfilled the purpose of the Old Testament. Thus, the promise of guidance into the truth was a promise of the securing for all time of the essential message of the Christian faith, which is what the New Testament provides. It certainly isn't a guarantee that every cock-eyed thought produced by well-meaning but un-informed Christians can be automatically attributed to the Holy Spirit and thus provide a shortcut to the meaning of the Bible.

G.W. Bromiley, 50 years ago, described the problem well. Speaking of the more extremist groups at the time of the Reformation, he says that they taught that 'the simple were better qualified to understand and follow the Bible than those whose minds were clouded by theological teaching... a doctrine of this kind was... intoxicating. Jack was even better than his master'.[6] Such an idea has always been attractive because it saves people the trouble of serious study: they can claim that 'God has told me', and that sounds supremely convincing to those who want easy solutions.

We must return to our tree symbol. Out of its trunk are the three great branches. The first is that of 'priest-hood', the second 'kingship' and the third 'prophecy'. We must now consider each of these in turn.

PRIESTS KINGS PROPHETS

COVENANT

GOD

THE BRANCH OF PRIESTHOOD

From the earliest recorded times, people have felt the need to offer sacrifice to their gods. This seems an almost universal practice and evidence for it has been provided from tribes and cultures all over the world. Mostly, the object of the sacrifice was an animal, but in some cultures it was a human being—a young man, a virgin, a child, a prisoner—all dying with much ceremonial.

The earliest record of a sacrifice in the Bible (Genesis 4:3–4) takes two forms. Cain offers grain—a cereal offering—the fruit of his work. Abel offers the choicest part of the firstborn lamb from his flock of sheep. This leads to murder, though the motive is not easy for us to understand.

The next reference to sacrifice relates to animals and birds and is Noah's mark of gratitude for the preservation of his family in the flood. He builds an altar and offers a burnt offering (Genesis 8:20).

In the patriarchal stories we are told of five altars built by Abraham, one by Isaac, and two by Jacob. It is reasonable to suppose that, in building these altars, each of the three patriarchs offered some kind of sacrifice, but only one 'burnt offering' is mentioned in connection with Abraham (the ram sacrificed in place of Isaac in Genesis 22:13) and two unspecified sacrifices are offered by Jacob without any reference to the building of an altar in either case (Genesis 31:54; 46:1).

What are we to infer from these patriarchal religious ritual places and acts? Quite simply that the head of the household or clan was responsible for such duties for hundreds of years throughout all the generations recorded in the book of Genesis, and that only one specific reference exists (Genesis 22:9–13) to indicate the nature of the sacrifices offered in all that time. Not once in the whole book of Genesis does a priest appear in connection with the patriarchal clan. Only one priest, Melchizedek, described as 'priest of El Elyon', appears in the briefest manner and with no reference to any role that he might have had of a priestly kind (Genesis 14:18–20). The only other priests are servants of pagan Egyptian gods in the era of Joseph's authority in Egypt. One was the father of Joseph's Egyptian wife and the others are merely mentioned as the landowners of an area of Egypt not sold to Pharaoh during the seven-year famine (Genesis 47:22, 26).

The first clear linkage of the Jewish people with the role of priesthood comes at Mount Sinai (Exodus 19:6) just three weeks after they had left Egypt, and the reference has immense significance. Moses is promised by God that if they keep the covenant and obey his voice they will be 'a priestly kingdom and a holy nation' as part of God's ownership of the 'whole earth'. The very phrase will be recalled some 1500 years later and applied in a new way to the followers of Jesus (1 Peter 2:9).

The books of Exodus and Leviticus set out the duties of a new and limited priesthood. The first priest was to be Aaron, Moses' brother, and the priestly caste was to be made up of his sons and their descendants. They were ordained in a ceremony of much splendour. They were clothed in special robes and were marked with the blood of a sacrificed ram on their ears, thumbs and big toes.

And what was their task? A whole series of daily sacrifices was to be initiated—sin-offerings, burnt offerings, grain offerings and various lesser offerings. All were to be made and a whole range of animals and birds were to be ritually slaughtered—bulls, rams, goats, sheep, lambs, doves and pigeons. As the letter to the Hebrews was, centuries later, to summarize the task, 'without the shedding of blood there is no forgiveness of sins' (9:22). The sacrifices were to take place and the resulting blood was to be dashed against the altar.

At the very heart of these rituals was an inner tent, curtained off, so holy that none might enter it except the high priest on one day each year, known as the Day of Atonement (*Yom Kippur*). What began as a two-roomed tent, with an outer 'Holy Place' and, behind the curtain, the 'Most Holy Place' (or 'Holy of Holies') was, centuries later, to be the focal point of King Solomon's temple. This inner room was an exact cube in measurement—three dimensions forming one entity. Some Christians, in due course, believed this to speak powerfully of the Trinity—three in one. On the annual Day of Atonement, the high priest was to take a bull and kill it. Then he entered the Most Holy Place through the curtain, taking incense which, burning, created a cloud, the symbol of God's mysterious presence, filling the tent. He took the bull's blood and sprinkled it before the mercy seat (the physical symbol of God's presence). Then he repeated the procedure with a goat. The bull was to be the sin offering for himself and his family while the goat fulfilled the same role for the whole nation of Israel.

So what was the purpose of this great daily blood-letting? Why was one day especially significant year by year? To the modern Western mind, the whole idea of blood-sacrifice is positively nauseating and makes no sense. How could it possibly have anything to do with spirituality? Isn't the word 'holiness' totally inappropriate for such butchery?

We need to pause at this point and clear our minds of prejudice. The first prejudice that we need to dispense with is the idea that human beings can breeze in on a holy God, say 'how're ya doin'?' and expect to be welcomed! Today's Westerners are so used to a self-centred lifestyle in which we do what we like and have no sense of absolute holiness and perfection that it is almost impossible for us to think of a divine being so morally perfect that we are utterly unfitted to come anywhere near him. Moses learned this lesson when God told him, 'No one shall see me and live' (Exodus 33:20). The Jewish prophets, faced with a vision of God's presence, all fell on their knees and pleaded their total unworthiness.

That's the first lesson. I am utterly unfitted to come close to God. Why? Because, to use the old-fashioned language, I am a sinner (Romans 3:23). This brings us to the second prejudice that we must dispose of. If God is too holy to come to easy terms with human sin, then I need to realize that sin, all sin, is worthy of death (Ezekiel 18:20; Romans 6:23). The purpose of the temple sacrificial system was to imprint indelibly on the Jewish mind the fact that the price of sin was the blood, the life-blood, of a innocent creature in my place (Hebrews 9:22). No sin was to be thought of as trivial and no forgiveness was to be made available 'on the cheap'. The seriousness of sin (the 'falling short' from God's perfection by disobedience or omission) was to be drilled into the mind of the Jew by the daily symbolism of the sacrificial system, initially in the movable tent and later in the magnificent temple. In each, the Most Holy Place, the sign of God's very presence, was never accessible to ordinary human beings because of their sin, and could be entered by the high priest only, acting on behalf of himself and the people. Even then he must carry the blood of the victim, the symbol of life laid down in death, as the price of forgiveness.

The covenant promise with Abraham (in our picture, the trunk of the tree) was then, through the branch of priesthood, first associated with human failure and sinfulness in all its universality. If God's promise to Abraham that, in his descendants, 'all the earth shall be blessed' was to have any meaning, then his family must themselves grasp the fundamental fact that all of them fell short of God through their sinfulness and self-centred pride, and that the cleansing and forgiveness of their sin required the death of an innocent animal. It could only ever be symbolic but the symbol was nevertheless a powerful reminder that, for the covenant promise to be effective, the initiative must come from God and the forgiveness can never be the reward of humanity's efforts but rather the acceptance of a gift provided by God at the cost of death—the death of an innocent.

One problem has always attached itself, however, to the idea of a formal priesthood. Historically, as Robert Brow has pointed out, priesthood 'always degenerated into the ugliness of priestcraft'.[7] He cites examples from India, Egypt, China, Persia and other lands where priestly roles turned into magic and ritualism. In most ancient cultures where priestcraft was dominant, 'a tidal wave of revolt... shattered the power of the old religions'. This resulted, Brow argued, in the appearance of 'seven world religions within fifty years of each other' and 'all continue to this day'.[8] The seven he cites are Zoroastrianism, Judaism, Buddhism, Jainism, Confucianism, Taoism and Vedanta Monism, all chiefly marked by an ethical revolt against the ritualism of the priestly order. The mere performance of religious ritual, minutely conforming to exact rules and words, has always been a corrupting influence, dominating the tradition of priestcraft and providing the temptation for ordinary people to believe that all that is needed by the gods is a stultifyingly accurate production of the 'right' words and ceremonial. Such ritual was to prove the object of scorn from the members of the third branch of the tree of the Abrahamic covenant, the prophets. In due course we shall examine that issue and the men who best reflect it in the history of the Jewish people.

The development of the priestly tradition in the Old Testament was, then, all part and parcel of the national covenant made by God with Moses and the emerging Jewish nation at Mount Sinai, immediately following the exodus from Egypt. Such a covenant was undoubtedly linked in its origin with the ancient covenant made with Abraham ('you shall be the ancestor of a multitude of nations'), but it was a covenant made with the Jewish people and in that sense limited to them. Interestingly, that national covenant is not described as an 'eternal' or 'everlasting' covenant in the two descriptions found in Exodus 24:7–8; 34:10, 27–28. We shall see in due course why this significant omission must be grasped.

THE BRANCH OF KINGSHIP

In the earliest period of Jewish history there were no kings. The nation was a 'theocracy', in other words, 'the Lord is king'. Incidentally, the biblical phrase 'the LORD' is an English title for what is known as the 'tetra-grammaton' (or 'four letters')—YHWH. These are the consonants that the Jews regarded as being too sacred to pronounce. Needing some way of saying the word, they combined these sacred consonants with the vowels of 'adonai' (which means 'my lord') and thus the tradition grew up of a sound like 'Jehovah'. In early Christian times, the Greek form became a sound 'iaoue', which was accepted as 'Yahweh'. Thus the personal name of God was taken to be Yahweh, meaning 'I am what I am' (or something of the kind!) and so 'Yahweh is king'. In the story of Moses and the burning bush (Exodus 3:2–15) the character of Yahweh is revealed for the first time, though the word, without any self-description, can be found throughout Genesis, sometimes on its own and at other times coupled with the word 'God'.

Throughout the nomadic period, as the Jews wandered around the desert of the Sinai peninsula (and north of it), Moses acted as judge until, at his father-in-law Jethro's suggestion, he appointed a group of able men to share the responsibility of leadership (Exodus 18:24–27). At his death, his lieutenant, Joshua, succeeded him. Joshua in turn was followed by an era in which leadership was taken over by a series of judges, for somewhere between 200 and 400 years (the length is disputed). The last of these judges was Samuel, who was the key figure for the final 20 years. For much of the period before Samuel there seems to have been anarchy (Judges 21:25) but he was widely respected until, in his old age, he appointed his two sons to succeed him. At that point the other Jewish leaders came to see him, complained that his sons were failing in their duties and said that the only solution was for the nation to be led by a king, as was the practice among the neighbouring countries (1 Samuel 8:5). Samuel was shocked by such a suggestion and replied that this was an indication that they had rejected God, despite his having brought them out of Egypt. Nevertheless God had instructed him to concede to their demands, to warn them of the conse-quences, and then to anoint a man of God's choice to be king. Samuel duly did this (1 Samuel 10:1) and in due course Saul was made the nation's first king (1 Samuel 10:20–24). A man physically head and shoulders above his fellows, personally courageous, yet three times disobedient to the known divine will, Saul was eventually and quite explicitly rejected from office and ultimately committed suicide after a military defeat. An alternative version of the account (2 Samuel 1:1–11) speaks of his actual despatch by an Amalekite, who found him dying and, at his request, finished him off.

Saul's successor, David, was to become the most famous of all the kings. Anointed by Samuel (1 Samuel 16:13) while Saul was still alive, his life story is highly dramatic and comprises high points, such as the defeat of the gigantic Goliath, and low points, such as his adultery with Bathsheba and the murder of her husband Uriah. The account of his life is one of the most detailed and lengthy records in the Bible, comprising 59 chapters in 1 and 2 Samuel, 1 and 2 Kings and 1 Chronicles. His name is associated with 71 Psalms and he is referred to nearly 60 times in the New Testament. In short, he is far and away the most important royal figure in the Old Testament.

As we have already seen, David received a promise through Nathan the prophet (2 Samuel 7:13, 16) that his kingdom and its throne will be 'established for ever' and David himself refers to this in his final oracle as 'an everlasting covenant' (2 Samuel 23:5). Doubtless, human history is littered with the dynastic hopes of powerful sovereigns who long to see the permanent perpetuation of their genes far into the future. Certainly, in the Jewish tradition David alone receives such a promise, though his son Solomon, on the occasion of the dedication of the Jerusalem temple, was aware that the promise had a qualification (1 Kings 8:25), namely 'if only your children look to their way, to walk before me as you have walked before me'.

renunciation of a religious faith

The continuing story of the monarchy contains many instances of 'the children' not keeping faith with Yahweh. Right from the building of the temple, there was apostasy. Solomon took hundreds of wives and concubines, some of whom 'turned away his heart after other gods; and his heart was not true to the Lord his God, as was the heart of his father David' (1 Kings 11:4). He built shrines to Astarte, Milcom, Chemosh and Molech, the local pagan deities, and 'the Lord was angry'. In consequence, Solomon received the divine judgment that because 'you have not kept my covenant... I will surely tear the kingdom from you... I will not do it in your lifetime; I will tear it out of the hand of your son'. Even so, the judgment was not absolute for 'I will not... tear away the entire kingdom; I will give one tribe to your son, for the sake of my servant David' (1 Kings 11:11–13).

Solomon's son, Rehoboam, acted foolishly and the promise came true. He lost all but the tribe of Judah (to which the tribe of Benjamin had become linked) and a new kingdom was created from the ten Israelite tribes, under Jeroboam (1 Kings 12:20–21). King after king 'did what was evil in the sight of the Lord' and eventually in 721BC the Assyrians, under Sargon, carried off nearly 28,000 of the population of the northern kingdom. These people vanished from recorded history.

Shortly before this cataclysm, Ahaz, king of Judah, had sought help from the Assyrian king, Tiglath-Pileser, who duly went on a campaign to rescue Ahaz from his local opponents. The price of this was the erection of a pagan altar in the Jerusalem temple, which functioned alongside the altar to Yahweh but clearly symbolized the fact that Judah had became a satellite province of Assyria (2 Kings 16:7–15). Isaiah the prophet, often thought to be himself of royal blood, protested, but to little avail.

Hezekiah, the son of Ahaz, was one of the few who, in the Bible's words, 'did what was right in the sight of the Lord' (2 Kings 18:3). As king, he smashed the pagan altars and idols, destroying the shrines and even breaking up the bronze 'serpent on the pole', which Moses had made (Numbers 21:9) as a symbol of Yahweh's healing power, since it had become itself a pagan idol in the people's worship. Even so, he was besieged in Jerusalem by the army of Assyrian king Sennacherib, Sargon's son, and all seemed lost (2 Kings 18:13). At this point, Isaiah prophesied that it was not Yahweh's intention that Jerusalem should fall and, by the morning, the sleeping Assyrian army was largely dead. It seems likely that bubonic plague or dysentery was the immediate cause. The story has been vividly retold by Byron in his poem, 'The destruction of Sennacherib', which famously begins, 'The Assyrian came down like a wolf on the fold' and tells of 'the Angel of Death' who 'breathed on the face of the foe' with the result that their might 'melted like snow in the glance of the Lord'.[9]

Hezekiah was followed by the long and evil reign of his son Manasseh, who, for over 40 years, undid all his father's good work, restoring the pagan altars in the temple. Eventually Manasseh's grandson, Josiah, came to the throne at the age of eight. When he was 20 he restored the temple as Hezekiah had done, pulling down idols and altars all across his kingdom, and, at the age of 26, began a programme of restoration and repair of the temple, using money that had been collected over some time for this purpose. During this operation a book (presumably a scroll) containing 'God's law' was discovered, which (though a source of controversy among scholars) is generally taken to have been a substantial part of Deuteronomy. Josiah read the document out to the leaders and people of the nation (2 Kings 23:2), which caused great shock. A reformation was set in motion and, although it seems not to have affected people's inner religious belief (they reverted to pagan practices on Josiah's death), a considerable impact was made on the religious and ritual practices of the time.

The southern kingdom of Judah, then, despite the serious attempts at religious revival under Hezekiah and Josiah, was still chiefly governed by kings who 'did what was evil'. In 597 and 582 two large deportations took place under the Babylonian king Nebuchadrezzar. The last of the kings of Judah, Zedekiah, whose fate it was to watch his sons slaughtered in front of him before his eyes were gouged out (Jeremiah 52:10–11), died in a Babylonian prison. The prophet Ezekiel exults in his end, calling him 'vile, wicked prince of Israel' and looks forward to one who will come 'whose right it is' to be king (Ezekiel 21:25, 27).

There, then, is the key to it all. Centuries earlier, Samuel had warned the Jews that the kings that they so desired would prove, generally, to be a bad lot. Such kings would build armies, take the people's land and use their sons as servants—whether as soldiers, farmers, or craftsmen—and their daughters as domestics. The king would also want their slaves, male and female, their animals and the best of their vineyards and orchards. In short, kings would use people, places and things for their own personal advantage and it would be too late for the Jews to complain because God would not listen (1 Samuel 8:11–18).

In the face of this concept (and reality) of monarchical life, an alternative expectation began to develop. It hinged on the matter of 'anointing' and came to focus on the word '*marshiac*', which we know as 'Messiah'. The word itself only occurs twice in the Old Testament, in the latest period, as part of the book of Daniel (9:25 and 26). Various interpretations as to who this figure might be have been offered down the years, including (linked to Isaiah 45:1) Cyrus the Persian and, obviously, Jesus of Nazareth.

While the Jewish people had always understood Yahweh to be the king, the succession of human kings for some 450 years had inevitably caused dissatisfaction with monarchy (as indeed Samuel had prophesied) and it was left to a small handful of prophets to look beyond the literal kingship to a concept of one within the Davidic line whose nature and character would be of an altogether more satisfying quality. This figure is explicitly to be found in the early chapters of Isaiah and, later, in one section of Jeremiah.

We look first at Isaiah 11 and see the opening up of the Davidic connection by the reference to David's father, Jesse (11:1). The tree imagery—its roots, its shoot and branch—locates the coming figure deep within David's line. He will be marked by the presence of the Spirit and will exhibit a series of qualities that come with that indwelling (Isaiah 11:2–5): as the Contemporary English Version has it, these will be 'understanding, wisdom and insight'. He will, it continues, 'be powerful, and he will know and honour the Lord' while 'his greatest joy will be to obey the Lord'. He 'won't judge by appearances or listen to rumours' since 'honesty and fairness will be his royal robes', and 'the poor and the needy will be treated... with justice' since 'his word will be law everywhere'. In consequence, 'just as water fills the sea, the land will be filled with people who know and honour the Lord'.

Jeremiah takes up the 'tree' language (33:15) and looks to the future. The Lord says, 'I promise that the time will come when I will appoint a king from the family of David, a king who will be honest and rule with justice' (CEV). The NRSV speaks of 'a righteous Branch' which will 'spring up for David'. Jerusalem, his city, will be called 'The Lord is our righteousness' (33:16).

The coming kingdom will have four characteristics. In the 1950s, John Stott identified them as standing out clearly. 'First, it would be just... secondly Messiah's reign would usher in peace... the third characteristic would be stability' while 'fourthly... it would be universal'.[10] Stott drew on relevant passages from Jeremiah 23:5–6; 1 Chronicles 22:6–10; 2 Samuel 7:10–16; Genesis 12:3 and Zechariah 9:10.

Anyone who has ever attended traditional Anglican Christmas carol services will almost certainly have heard Isaiah 9:6–7 read year by year. It perfectly summarizes the four qualities of the coming kingdom. The passage reads:

> *A child has been born for us,*
> *a son given to us;*
> *authority rests upon his shoulders;*
> *and he is named*
> *Wonderful Counsellor (just ruler),*
> *Mighty God (universal dominion),*
> *Everlasting Father (stability),*
> *Prince of Peace (peace).*
> *His authority shall grow continually,*
> *and there shall be endless peace*
> *for the throne of David and his kingdom.*
> *He will establish and uphold it*
> *with justice and with righteousness*
> *from this time onwards and for evermore.*
> *The zeal of the Lord of hosts will do this.*

Faced with such an understanding of the kingdom and its king, those disillusioned by the Jewish monarchies have at last something to look forward to. This is what the theologians call 'the messianic hope'.

After their return from exile in Babylon, the idea of a coming Messiah began to grow within the Jewish community. His Davidic roots, his authority, his provision of justice and peace, all seemed to indicate a military ruler who would free the nation from outside oppression. Whether this oppression came from Persian, Greek, Egyptian, Syrian or Roman sources (and it did at various times come from all of them), Messiah would appear to save the nation as God's chosen, anointed deliverer. Various contenders for the title were suggested. In the decades before and after the birth of Jesus, two attempts at revolt were launched by, first, Theudas and, second, Judas (Acts 5:36–37), but both were easily put down. Either or both may have been messianic pretenders. The Dead Sea scrolls include the expectation of a Messiah and a time of 'messianic rule'.

The branch of kingship, then, was a strange mixture of divine intention and the human need to 'keep up with the Joneses' in the next Palestinian valley and hill. The latter motive combined also with the need to get some kind of law and order in an era when everyone did 'what they thought was right' (Judges 21:25, CEV). Such a recipe for anarchy has always appealed to those who are foolish enough to think that a just and peaceful society can be built on the supposed natural good will of humanity. History tells a very different story.

Nevertheless, the story of kingship, while offering plenty of support for the warnings pronounced by the prophet Samuel, was also the seedbed from which the concept of a 'kingdom of God'—just, peaceful, universal, and permanent—came to enshrine a messianic hope which was to lie at the heart of the Jewish expectation during the final years of the Old Testament.

Even so, a third force was to play a highly significant role alongside those of the priests and kings, which was far more confrontational than the first two.

THE BRANCH OF PROPHECY

There have always been prophets. They have, says H.L. Ellison, 'existed from the very first'.[11] Even those whom we do not normally associate with the title 'prophet' have been thus described. The earliest character so mentioned is Enoch (the second of that name), the seventh generation from Adam (Genesis 5:18–24), who is said by the New Testament author Jude to have 'prophesied' (Jude 14). The reference is to the book of Enoch, a Jewish non-canonical book (one that is not in the Bible) which was obviously known in the late first century, and which Jude quotes freely.

Abraham is described as a prophet (Genesis 20:7), as is Moses (Deuteronomy 18:15), and the term is not restricted to the Jewish people. Balaam, who came from what today we would call Iraq, is so described (2 Peter 2:16) and his religious affiliation is somewhat confused. Certainly prophets in the Bible are by no means reliable as authentic voices. The 'false prophet' was a regular feature in Israel, as were the 'court prophets' who surrounded kings and made all the right noises to order. Not surprisingly, these men were popular with the king of the day. That situation has always been the case: say what the monarch wants to hear and you will be flavour of the month. Inevitably, then, the prophet of Yahweh, whoever he was, was liable to be in head-on collision with the king and the sycophants who have always clustered around the key figures in a king's household.

What, then, was the role of the true prophet, the prophet of Yahweh? Ellison points out that he 'was not defined or explained in the Old Testament' but was simply 'taken for granted'.[12] What is more, the popular idea that the prophet is someone who foretells the future like some bogus fairground stargazer is alien to the thought of the Bible. Instead, his task is to be God's spokesman. Such speaking for Yahweh may sometimes involve foretelling the future but this is a secondary, not a primary, duty. When it does happen, it is never intended either to satisfy idle human curiosity or even to demonstrate that God knows the future but rather to help us interpret God's activity the better for its having been foretold.

The prophet, then, speaks primarily to his own day and the message springs out of the circumstances in which he lives. Even so, the message is not merely a common-sense application of wisdom, knowledge and human brain-power. It comes directly from God, reveals the purposes of an unchanging God and has a depth beyond the prophet's own understanding of it (see 1 Peter 1:10–12).

Throughout a great deal of the Old Testament, a tension existed between the kings and priests on the one hand and the prophets on the other. The former created an alliance of church and state, supporting and appointing each other in the joint social and religious aspects of society. Quite often kings appointed priests and priests anointed kings, binding themselves together as a political and religious unit. In the nature of things, it paid both to keep on good terms with each other. While the strengths of such a union have been obvious throughout history in the maintenance of the status quo and the blessing of war when required, the need for some kind of challenge was both necessary and, at the same time, a distinct threat to the joint establishment of king and priest. This was, inevitably, the role of the prophet. He was Yahweh's voice, directing, urging and warning and standing firm, whatever the cost, over against the corrupting influence of false prophets who merely endorsed the expectations, intentions and actions of the kings and priests. The former fulfilled the monarchical characteristics of which Samuel warned the people when they first called for a king to lead them (1 Samuel 8), while the latter placed ritual far above ethical behaviour as Micah was to complain (Micah 6:6–8), creating a system of sacrificial worship which satisfied the consciences of the people by repeated animal offerings unaccompanied by any form of behaviour that put love of God and neighbour in first place.

So who were the Old Testament prophets? There is bound to be an assumption that they are the men who have biblical books named after them. Thus Isaiah, Jeremiah and Ezekiel (whose books are the largest) are 'major prophets' and a collection of twelve (shorter) 'minor prophets' follow. In the biblical order, they are Hosea, Joel, Amos, Obadiah, Jonah, Micah, Nahum, Habakkuk, Zephaniah, Haggai, Zechariah and Malachi. Interestingly, the one omitted figure is Daniel, whom the Jews did not regard as a prophet. His book is usually described as 'apocalyptic' and is not placed with either the historical or prophetic books in the Jewish Bible.

As we have already seen, this list does not include

other important figures such as Abraham, Moses, Samuel, Nathan, Elijah, Elisha, and many others who remain unnamed. On one occasion (1 Kings 18:4), one hundred of Yahweh's prophets were hidden in two caves by King Ahab's chief steward to protect them from the murderous intentions of the king's pagan wife, Jezebel. Some at least of the more significant prophets gathered groups of disciples around them in prophetic schools.

Some of the leading prophets were not only public speakers; they also intended their words to be recorded. This does not seem to have been the case with Samuel, Elijah and Elisha, very few of whose words have come to us. By contrast, the words of Isaiah, Jeremiah and Ezekiel have evidently been recorded. As regards Jeremiah, he was himself aware that a collection of his utterances was needed and he dictated his warnings to Baruch, his amanuensis and secretary (Jeremiah 36:4). This scroll was destroyed by order of King Jehoiakim and a second augmented version was written, again at Jeremiah's dictation.

As regards Isaiah, there is a clear suggestion that some of his work should be recorded by some unnamed person or group on a tablet or book (Isaiah 30:8). Since books, in the modern sense, did not exist at the time, presumably a scroll is meant. The instruction may well (as in 8:16) be directed to a group of the prophet's disciples, to whom the message is to be entrusted for safekeeping.

The second section of Isaiah's prophecy (widely known as 'Deutero-Isaiah') is, according to Ellison, 'written rather than spoken prophecy'[13] and contains 'the most sustained poetry in the prophetic books'. He goes on to suggest that 'the message in its totality only became clear to the prophet himself as he received and recorded it'.[14] We shall return to this part of the prophecy in due course to see some of the most important and profound words in the whole of the Old Testament.

The prophet Ezekiel's work was described a century ago by J. Skinner as 'arranged on a plan so perspicuous and so comprehensive that the evidence of literary design in the composition becomes altogether irresistible'.[15] A.B. Davidson had just previously taken a similar view, arguing that it 'was issued in its complete form at once'.[16] These views have been challenged but more recently reasserted by J.B. Taylor and others cited by him.[17]

Clearly, then, some of the major prophetic utterances were recorded in writing, so the idea that for prophecy to be authentic it must be pronounced in some ecstatic way, with the prophet having no awareness of its meaning, cannot stand up to examination. Undoubtedly there were instances of ecstatic experience among the prophets. Almost unique among these was the brief ecstatic occasion following Saul's anointing to be king (1 Samuel 10:10), since he was not intended to be a prophet as such but rather a monarch and ruler. As to both Isaiah and Ezekiel, each had some kind of ecstatic vision, Isaiah of Yahweh enthroned in the temple and Ezekiel of Yahweh's glory in the storm during Israel's exile in Babylon. Ecstatic frenzy was certainly a characteristic of Canaanite Baal worship and has often been induced during dancing and chanting but there is very little suggestion that this was a characteristic of Jewish prophetic experience. Neither of the visions recorded of Isaiah's and Ezekiel's awareness of Yahweh's presence suggest any kind of frenzy but rather a deep sense of awe.

One other area of prophetic behaviour must be noted. All three of the major prophets were involved in what has come to be called 'acted oracles'. The hostility with which the prophets were received led in all three cases to their seeking to capture public attention. Isaiah went naked and barefoot for three years. Jeremiah accepted the call not to marry (a rare course of action for a Jew); he took and broke a pottery jug, wore a wooden yoke, purchased a field, offered wine to the teetotal Rechabites, and sank a stone, with an attached message, in the Euphrates. Ezekiel acted out the siege of Jerusalem, went on a food ration of bread and water, prepared a shoulder-bag to go on the exiles' journey, and faced his wife's death without mourning. In addition, the minor prophet Hosea was instructed to marry a prostitute, yet another of the prophetic acted oracles. All these were symbolic warnings and, once seen, were explained to the watchers. In short, the prophets took every available means, obeying God's commands, to ram home the divine displeasure at human behaviour, especially that of the Jewish people in their disobedience.

This brings us to the most important element of all the prophetic utterances, namely the strange and mysterious figure introduced in the second part of Isaiah. Four so-called 'Servant Songs' begin with chapter 42. The passages in question are very widely recognized and accepted as providing a coherent sequence, even though they are embedded in a wider section, namely chapters 40—55. The four passages are of unequal length, being 42:1-4; 49:1-6; 50:4-9; and 52:13—53:12. We must now consider them carefully for they have come to have an importance far outweighing their meagre 31 verses. Within the branch of prophecy, they occupy a crucial (in every sense of that word) position.

'Look', says Yahweh through the voice of his prophet, 'here is my servant' (Isaiah 42:1). He goes on to say that the Servant is his chosen one, one whom he has (as J.A. Motyer says) 'gripped fast'[18] and who greatly pleases him. Yahweh's Spirit empowers him, enabling him to bring justice to the nations. At once, both the covenant with Abraham is recalled and the linkage is made with one in whom all the nations will be blessed. So too the memory goes back to the coming Messiah promised in Isaiah 9:7, who will establish his kingdom with justice.

The Servant, however, is no military king. His voice is gentle, his manner is calm and caring, his 'quiet, un-aggressive, unthreatening ministry' is, in C.R. North's words, 'without precedent'.[19] He has a task to fulfil and, says Motyer, 'the pressures and blows that immobilise others will not deter him'.[20] The world is waiting for his teaching.

So who is this Servant? There seem to be three possibilities. The exiled Jews in Babylon, not to mention their Babylonian masters, are all aware that Cyrus, the king of Persia, is moving inexorably towards the city (which he will, in due course, conquer) and their future is extremely uncertain. Yet, amazingly, Isaiah (44:28; 45:1) speaks of him as Yahweh's anointed, his chosen shepherd, who will carry out all his purpose. Both titles have strong messianic overtones ('shepherd' had had kingly overtones since David began as a shepherd boy). Can he be the promised servant? The first Servant Song makes this extremely unlikely. Cyrus may indeed, in the providence of God, have fulfilled a role in the divine purposes but Isaiah describes him as 'a bird of prey' (46:11). Cyrus was indeed one of a long line of Middle Eastern tyrants, by no means lacking in certain positive qualities as a ruler but hardly 'quiet, unaggressive and unthreatening' with gentle, calm and caring virtues. Cyrus may indeed have been, probably unwittingly, a pawn in God's historical chess-game but he clearly doesn't fit the task for which Isaiah's Servant has been set apart by Yahweh.

The second candidate for the Servant's role is Israel, the nation. Indeed, in the second of the Servant Songs, Yahweh actually announces, 'You are my servant, Israel, in whom I will be glorified' (49:3). This is an interesting solution, although it poses real problems. In Isaiah (41:14), Yahweh speaks in disparaging terms of 'Jacob you worm and Israel you maggot' (REB), which hardly seems a natural introduction to the idea that Israel, the nation, is Yahweh's Servant. How, then, can Israel possibly be the Servant prophesied?

Motyer offers an interpretation which has a good deal

to commend it. Israel was 'the name of an individual before it became a national name'.[21] That individual was Jacob, Abraham's grandson, and he was one of the patriarchs to whom the divine covenant was reiterated. Thus, in Isaiah's prophecy, following the disparaging remarks about Isaiah the nation, the Servant mentioned is, instead, Israel the patriarch, one of those to whom the eternal covenant was endorsed in its earliest days. The 'outward Israel does not have the real Israel's characteristics', in John Goldingay's words.[22]

This still leaves us, however, with the problem that Israel is called 'a maggot', and Jacob is described as 'a worm'. Both names refer initially to the same man, even though Jacob's name was changed to Israel (Genesis 32:28). 'Jacob' meant 'the supplanter' (Genesis 27:36) whereas Israel meant 'God strives' or 'one who strives with God' following the wrestling match between Jacob and the mysterious man whom Jacob believed to be God (Genesis 32:30). If the Servant Songs have any direct relationship to the Jewish nation, and there are certainly some indications that this might be so, there are still further indications that point to a specific individual. So who might that be?

We must look further at Songs 2, 3 and 4. Whereas song 1 comes from the voice of Yahweh, in Song 2 it is the Servant who speaks (Isaiah 49:1–6). He addresses the distant nations, describing his call from the time when he was in the womb, where he was named. From then onwards he was quietly prepared for his life's work, sharpened and polished yet concealed in readiness for the right time. Nevertheless, the Servant feels depressed because his work seems unappreciated, but he continues to trust in Yahweh and the fulfilment yet to come. The task is even bigger than he had first assumed. Not only the nation of Israel is to be restored but also he must reach out to the whole world, bringing light to far-off nations.

The third Song (Isaiah 50:4–9) continues the Servant's voice as he describes his continued preparation for his ministry, which will involve teaching others and encouraging those whose hopes are at a low ebb. Despite this, he remains unloved and suffers hatred, persecution and violence but continues to trust in Yahweh who will vindicate him. So he goes on facing up to opposition, knowing that he will ultimately outlast them.

Lastly comes Song 4, which is a painful story of ongoing rejection (Isaiah 52:12—53:12). Yahweh is once more the speaker who rejoices that the Servant will be triumphant but not until he has become the Suffering Servant, so horribly mangled that he is hardly recognized as a human being. Even rulers will be silenced by the sight of what happens.

One more Yahweh retells the story of the Servant. The man is unknown, born and brought up in obscurity with no glamour or importance that might attract people to him. Thus it is his fate to be rejected, despised, sorrowing and suffering, treated with scorn and disdain. Why should this be? While humanity sees him as God-forsaken, his real task is to bear their sins and the force of the righteous judgment that is rightly theirs. We human beings go our own way like a flock of straying sheep and Yahweh's just punishment falls upon him, the innocent one. So the story grinds on. The Suffering Servant, like a sacrificial lamb, stays silent up to the time of his death and then he is laid in a tomb despite his personal honesty and gentleness.

The song is almost over. Most terrible of all, it is Yahweh himself who fulfils his own will in this sacrifice, so that the Suffering Servant might be humanity's sin-offering, bringing hope and salvation to all who accept the benefit of his self-offering as their sin-bearer who alone can make them righteous. The awesome deed completed, Yahweh can now reward him for his faithful acceptance of his role as saviour of both Jew and Gentile—the many who gratefully acknowledge him as the true Servant who has interceded for them even at the point of his most fearsome agony. The Servant has triumphed.

The highest point of the prophetic task has been reached, and it remains for the identity of the Servant to be revealed. Who can it be? Not Cyrus. Nor Israel, though that nation will face many of the Servant's horrific experiences. The children of Abraham, the people of the eternal covenant, must wait. All will be revealed—but not yet.

So the great branches coming out of the trunk of the covenant tree of promise have opened up to us the triple range of themes contained in the Old Testament. Priest, king, and prophet have all appeared and set out their stalls. As the centuries pass, the Jewish people watch their temples being destroyed and rebuilt, their kings rising and falling, their prophets continually challenging and warning and pointing forward to a coming fulfilment of all their hopes. Messiah will come. He will come. His promise will not fail.

THE TREE OF LIFE

The shape of our tree, its trunk and its three great branches is now clear enough. The promise is perceived by the Jewish people as being their promise, made by Yahweh to Abraham and his descendants—and that means them. Surrounded as they had been for virtually all their history by hostile tribes and empires, carried off into exile in Babylon and, from their return onwards, deprived of kings, having to rebuild a new and much less impressive temple, and with few significant prophetic figures, the nation becomes increasingly ghetto-like, deeply suspicious of all things Gentile, though living among Gentiles, frequently as a vassal-state, effectively controlled by empire after empire.

Sixty or so years before the birth of Jesus of Nazareth, Pompey the Great, one of Rome's First Triumvirate (the others being Crassus and Julius Caesar) annexed Palestine and, after a siege, took Jerusalem. According to Josephus, the Jewish historian, he entered the temple 'and saw all that which it was unlawful for any other men to see, but only for the high priests'.[23] Over one hundred years earlier, Antiochus IV (called 'Epiphanes'), a Seleucid king, had desecrated the very Holy of Holies, leading to the Maccabean revolt in 165BC when Judas Maccabaeus recaptured Jerusalem and cleansed the temple of the pagan altar brought in by Antiochus. Pompey, says Josephus to his credit, 'touched nothing… on account of his regard to religion', acting in 'a manner… worthy of his virtue.[24]

Two decades after the annexation of Palestine, the Romans appointed Herod (the Great) as king of Judea, which he ruled on behalf of Rome until his death in 4BC. Not, as we have seen, being of pure Jewish blood and certainly not from the Davidic line, he was hated and despised by the Jews for his systematic murder of the Hasmonean dynasty (who had taken over the high priesthood), culminating in the murder of Mariamne, one of his wives, who came from that family. Herod commenced the building of a hugely grandiose temple in 19BC (not completed until AD64) to ingratiate himself with the Jewish people.

It was into this world of Herod the Great, a ruler of great political vision and shrewdness and yet a cruel butcher who killed a wife and two or more sons, that a baby was conceived in the town of Nazareth. The two accounts in Matthew 1:18–25 and, more fully, in Luke 1:26–56 speak of Mary, a virgin, and her husband-to-be, Joseph, being stunned by the message brought to them: this conception is unique, since the child is to be 'a saviour' (the meaning of the name 'Yeshua' or, in Greek, 'Jesus') and the one who will occupy 'the throne of his ancestor David' (Luke 1:31–32). Mary's song of wonder, the Magnificat, identifies all this as the work of Yahweh, who long ago made a promise 'to our ancestors, to Abraham and to his descendants for ever' (Luke 1:55).

At the infant's birth, the message to the Bethlehem shepherds reinforces the meaning. The child born in the town, the 'city of David', will be 'a saviour, who is the Messiah' (Luke 2:11). Six weeks later, an old man, Simeon, living in Jerusalem, is shown the baby in the temple and, having had a divine revelation that he 'would not see death before he had seen the Lord's Messiah', recognizes the infant as Yahweh's 'salvation', who will be 'glory to... Israel' and 'a light for revelation to the Gentiles' (Luke 2:26, 30, 32).

Luke adds a further valuable piece of information. He begins his Gospel not with Jesus, but with the conception and birth of John the Baptist, whose mother, Elizabeth, was related to Mary (Luke 1:36) and whose father, Zechariah, was a priest. Elizabeth, on Mary's arrival to stay with her when both are pregnant, speaks of her as 'the mother of my Lord' (an extraordinary phrase for a much older woman to use of a young virgin and one which clearly has messianic overtones). As for Zechariah, he, as a priest, links his son John's birth to a coming saviour from the kingly Davidic line, who will fulfil the covenant with Abraham. John will be a prophetic forerunner going before Messiah, and will thus be able to see the fulfilment of Isaiah's prophecy of the one who will 'give light to those who sit in darkness' (Luke 1:79; Isaiah 9:2).

In quoting these words, Luke sees the connection between the Abrahamic covenant, the messianic kingdom, the prophetic ministry and the priestly task. Thus his Gospel brings all together in relation to the arrival of Jesus, Messiah and saviour, on the scene.

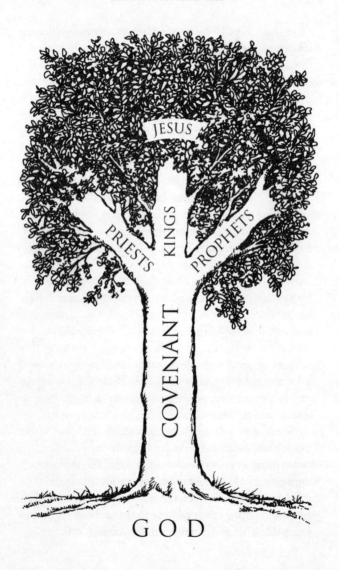

The Old Testament, as we have recognized, introduces us to the eternal covenant and then, in historical sequence, brings before us first the priesthood, then the kingdom, and lastly the prophetic Servant. Now, as we move into the New Testament, the order changes. The Gospels are dominated by the kingdom, then the Servant, and only briefly by the priestly work. The Abrahamic covenant is hardly mentioned. After the death and resurrection of Jesus, Acts and the letters say little explicitly about the kingdom, but develop the Servant theme and that of the covenant until, finally, the letter to the Hebrews reveals in great detail the priestly role that Jesus played. We must, then, now pursue this development in the sequence in which it occurs and, in due course, see its implications for the whole Christian Church.

THE BRANCH OF KINGSHIP: JESUS THE MESSIAH

The three synoptic Gospels—Matthew, Mark, and Luke —all introduce the story of the adult Jesus with the ministry of his relative, John the Baptist. Both begin their preaching with identical words, namely, 'Repent, for the kingdom of heaven has come near.'

This idea of a divine kingdom is, as we have seen, one of the most crucial themes in both Old and New Testaments. In the former it develops from the prophetic response to the failure of the monarchy, while in the latter it is the key theme relating to the work of Messiah (in Greek, 'Christ', meaning the anointed one). The word 'kingdom' appears 55 times in Matthew's Gospel, 19 times in Mark, 45 times in Luke but only four times in John.

The Jews clearly expected the promised Messiah to eject the Romans and rule in majesty. The role model for this was King David. It wasn't surprising, then, that when the young Galilean, Jesus, appeared on the scene in or about the year AD27, his preaching was heavily focused on the theme of the kingdom.

By far the most famous sermon preached by Jesus was what we call 'The Sermon on the Mount', recorded in Matthew 5—7. It is hugely misunderstood by large numbers of people who, largely relying on a mixture of Hollywood and televised accounts of the life of Jesus, assume that he got up on to a hill and shouted solemnly to a large crowd, mouthing a lot of pious platitudes that sound impressive. People often say, 'I do so like the Sermon on the Mount' and are amazed when I say, 'Really? It horrifies me. It is so appallingly demanding and aims to turn my whole world upside down.' They haven't understood what it's all about and have latched on to a few beautiful phrases in archaic language. 'Blessed are the pure in heart' only sounds nice to those who haven't begun to examine the inner thoughts and wishes of their own consciences. Anyone who does so will soon realize how far from 'pure' is the average human heart, riddled with pride, selfishness, greed, lust and a whole host of unattractive characteristics.

We must begin, then, by seeking to discover where and to whom the sermon was preached, and what it was about. Clearly it was on a hill (Matthew 5:1) but it wasn't delivered standing, to a great audience. Jesus sat down and, like a Jewish rabbi, he began to teach his immediate followers, his 'disciples' (5:2). The crowd was able to overhear something of what he said (7:28), for they recognized his authority, but his words were aimed at those who were disciples, not gawping hangers-on. As to what he said, it was clearly his explanation of the ideals and outworking of the kingdom. Eight times he refers to 'the kingdom' and its members, its qualities, the need to seek it and enter it. We must examine this sermon more carefully, for it is the Magna Carta of the faith, the great charter of the kingdom of God.

Jesus begins by talking of the marks of true happiness. The traditional Bible versions in English use the word 'blessed', but most people have no idea what that word, which sounds very pious, actually means. The Greek text says *makarioi* and it means 'happiness' or 'the happy ones'. In Luke's version there are just four 'happy' conditions. If you are destitute, starving, sobbing and hated, then you are '*makarioi*'. According to Luke, Jesus taught starkly that the kingdom was about turning the world's values upside down. To be a member of the kingdom is to find joy and fulfilment when you have rejected the lifestyle of the world and have been, in consequence, rejected by the world yourself. That, says Jesus, is how and when you find true happiness. Matthew's account is gentler but it still declares that happiness results from possessing the inner virtues which are generally in conflict with society's attitudes and goals. Weakness, gentleness, mercy, longing for holiness, regret for one's sinful and

disobedient attitudes, and willingness to be misunderstood and persecuted—how rarely are these thought to
be desirable qualities! Yet, to Jesus, these are what the
kingdom is all about. These are its ideals and he himself
exhibited them, which was why he was ultimately
'despised and rejected'. This wasn't the kind of Messiah
the nation was looking for, thank you very much. Jesus
uses the illustrations of salt and light to reinforce his
points: salt purifies and adds flavour; light banishes
darkness and reveals what is hidden.

The sermon then goes on to demonstrate how these
ideals relate to the Old Testament attitudes to murder,
adultery, oath taking, the question of retribution and
enmity towards other people (5:17–48). Always it is the
inner motivation and not just the outward act that distinguishes the kingdom's members. Jesus turns next to the
religious practices of his nation, citing almsgiving, prayer
and fasting (6:1–18), and again stresses the inward nature,
not the outward ostentation that so often takes its place.

His third area of illustration concerns the problems
of everyday life. Avarice, anxiety and accusation (6:19—
7:12) are all challenged by kingdom ideals, showing the
need for insight, intercession and inter-dependence.

Lastly, he announces that the kingdom demands
action. It is not about solemn 'spirituality' and high-
thinking. It only leads anywhere if the imperatives are
obeyed: we must 'enter' it through a narrow gate. There
are two ways, two kinds of fruits and two destinations.
Only one of each brings happiness and real fulfilment. A
safe house needs solid foundations and the only true rock
is Jesus' teaching.

One of the most vivid and memorable aspects of the teaching that Jesus presents is the way he uses stories (parables) to make his points stick. Unfortunately, as he himself was only too aware, most people, while remembering the stories, don't grasp their meaning (Matthew 13:11–13). Certainly, as far as the dozen or more parables recorded by Matthew go, the goal of each one is to help Jesus' hearers, and especially the disciples, to understand what 'the kingdom of heaven' is like. Churches even today are full of people who have heard of the sower, the mustard seed, the pearl of great price, the wise and foolish bridesmaids, the labourers in the vineyard and so on, but have little or no idea what their point is. People often wish clergy would 'tell stories like Jesus did', but when I once told a 'parable of the block of flats' (which had a very pungent and vivid message) most of the congregation had no idea what it meant. When Jesus said 'Let anyone with ears listen!' he clearly knew that few could or would.

A sermon, a set of parables—yes, and a whole series of signs. We tend to call them miracles and are greatly tempted to assume that Jesus was a bit like a magic circle magician who says 'And now for my next trick'. Sadly, to think like that is to fail to see what the miracles are all about.

What greatly helps me is to discover that John the Baptist, in prison shortly before his murder by Herod Antipas, sent some of his followers to Jesus to ask him quite directly whether he was, in fact, Messiah. Jesus sent a reply to John which would have made complete sense to both of them. He cited various passages from

Isaiah which referred to the actions of Messiah: 'the blind receive their sight, the lame walk, the lepers are cleansed, the deaf hear, the dead are raised, the poor have good news brought to them' (Luke 7:22). John would recognize only too well that his question was answered. These 'signs' were the prophesied marks of the coming Messiah. As 'miracles', they were no mere clever tricks to show off personal power. Every one was a significant action, messianic in its own right.

Later, when Jesus was on trial, he was sent to face Herod Antipas, John's murderer. Herod, we are told by Luke, was pleased because he was hoping to see Jesus 'perform some sign'. In the presence of the one who had killed his relative John, there was no way that Jesus would perform to order; nor indeed would he even deign to speak to him or answer any of his questions. Jesus was no performing monkey, out to please the local potentate by a show of his miraculous gifts (Luke 23:8–10).

The pivotal point in Matthew's Gospel (16:13–20) comes when Jesus and his disciples have travelled 25 miles north of the sea of Galilee to a pagan town, formerly a Greek centre of Pan-worship, recently re-named Caesarea Philippi. Prior to this, Jesus has regularly told those whom he healed not to speak of it, since this would have led to increasing speculation that he was indeed the promised Messiah. Now, far from Jewish towns and villages, he opens up the subject with his little group of disciples. 'Who do people say that the Son of Man is?' (The title 'Son of Man' was an ambiguous one which could mean anything from 'man' to 'Messiah'). They give him a series of improbable answers currently circulating. 'But who do you,' he asks more pointedly, 'say that I am?' Peter boldly replies, 'You are the Messiah, the Son of the living God.' This was, for a Jew, virtual blasphemy, but Jesus congratulates Peter, declaring that such an understanding came not from human thought but from God the Father in heaven. Such a confession of faith, he adds, is the rock on which he would build his Church. In using this word, '*ecclesia*', for the first (and almost the only) time, Jesus introduces the idea that he has a specific community of believers in mind, namely those who acknowledge him as truly the promised Messiah.

Even so, at this climactic point, he instructs his disciples 'not to tell anyone that he was the Messiah' (16:20). In due course they travel to Jerusalem, down the Jordan valley to Jericho and then up the long climb to the capital. Before leaving Jericho, a remarkable event takes place. Matthew, Mark and Luke all record the anguished cry of one or two blind men seeking the restoration of their sight. They address Jesus as 'Son of David', which clearly indicates that they understand him to have messianic pretensions. A few days later, as he enters the city, what Matthew describes as 'a very large crowd' (21:8) uses the same phrase, as do various children within the temple (21:15), presumably repeating what they have already heard the adults shouting.

Perhaps more remarkable still was the occasion (15:21–22), much earlier, while Jesus was in the Gentile area of Phoenicia, some 50 miles north of Nazareth, when he was accosted by a local woman seeking exorcism for her daughter. She, too, used the title 'Son of David'. It was, by any standard, a strange description for a pagan woman to use, but it clearly indicated that the idea of a coming messianic figure, a descendant of King David, was not unknown even outside the Jewish community. This event, incidentally, preceded Peter's acknowledgment of Jesus as the Messiah at Caesarea Philippi.

The ministry of Jesus comes to a head in the week preceding Passover, in Jerusalem. Once more the messianic issue is at the heart of his collision with the religious authorities. Following his arrest, he is interrogated by Caiaphas, the high priest, who puts him on oath, asking, 'Are you the Messiah?' (Matthew 26:63; Mark 14:61). The answer Jesus gives, while seemingly ambiguous, is effectively an acknowledgment that he is, since the text quoted from Daniel (7:13–14) was a well-recognized messianic prophecy.

Taken before Pilate, the Roman procurator, he is asked whether he is 'king of the Jews'. Clearly the high priest had used the messianic admission in its most political sense in his request to Pilate for justice. To a Roman, the language could only be construed as a claim to challenge the emperor's authority. Despite his weak behaviour under pressure, Pilate's treatment of Jesus takes the 'kingly' role in a literalistic way. In consequence, his soldiers crown Jesus with thorns, put a royal robe on him, give him a reed as a parody of a sceptre and do mock homage to him. The charge against him, 'King of the Jews', is set above him on the cross, which becomes his royal throne. Finally, the priests and leaders join in the mockery, calling on 'the Messiah, the King of Israel' to come down from the cross.

So, the King of Israel, the Messiah, Jesus of Nazareth, gets his royal throne. The kingdom has arrived. The prophecies have been fulfilled. A few weeks later, the apostle Peter is preaching unashamedly before the Sanhedrin that he is a witness, as are they, that 'God... raised up Jesus, whom you had killed by hanging him on a tree' (Acts 5:30)—a theme that he took up again 30 years later in his first letter, declaring that Jesus 'bore our sins in his body on the tree' (1 Peter 2:24). Finally, John, in the Revelation, brings Christ's death as a lamb into conjunction with what is now 'the tree of life' (Revelation 22:2) close by the heavenly throne.

The kingdom has, in Jesus, found its ultimate meaning. The promise to David of an eternal covenant in which one of his successors will be seated on the throne has been finally fulfilled. The King of kings and Lord of lords will reign for ever.

THE BRANCH OF PROPHECY:
JESUS THE SERVANT

Some years ago I gave a series of lectures in the USA about 'Jesus, the Servant'. I stressed that the idea found especial focus in its fulfilment of the famous Isaiah 53 passage with its description of the 'Suffering Servant'. Weeks later a man telephoned me. 'This Servant', he said. 'Is he in the Bible?' I was somewhat stunned, considering the amount of time I had given to explaining the matter. Then came the shattering response. 'Well, he's never been mentioned in any church I've ever attended.' Sadly, having been to the States on twelve occasions in the last 25 years, I have to admit that I have never heard the idea mentioned in any church there. Nor, for that matter, has it been on the agenda of many English churches in that same period, especially in the Evangelical tradition.

Why is that? I suspect that most Christians don't much like hearing about pain, torture and death and greatly prefer to think about the triumphant aspect of the resurrection and the powerful impact of the Holy Spirit—talking and singing about 'winning' without ever facing actual suffering for their faith. Our churches in the West can be dominated by the kingly, triumphalist kind of imperial faith that must be seen to pull in the crowds and offer excitement to all in the name of Jesus. This kind of faith is summarized in terms of success in the three areas of 'dollars, bricks and souls'. Pull in the dollars, pile high the bricks, and save the souls. It is, in short, a kind of supermarket religion where all good Christians win and all shall have prizes. You don't even need to be committed to the extreme version of the so-called 'prosperity gospel' to find yourself deeply entrenched in the 'success' version of the Christian faith.

But—and it's a very big but—that kind of Christianity is a caricature, avoiding (as Peter long ago tried to avoid) the Suffering Servant element that is a crucial part of the life and work of Jesus.

We must, then, make a real attempt to understand the Servant element that characterizes the teaching and behaviour of Jesus. To do that, we have to return and remind ourselves of those so-called Servant passages in the prophecy of Isaiah.

The first (Isaiah 42:1–4), you recall, introduced 'my servant', who is chosen by God, pleasing to God, empowered by God's Spirit—a gentle, caring man who looks kindly on the bruised and needy. He is not a man given to shouting his wares in public but his goal is justice for the world, for whom he has a message.

This first 'Servant Song' is fulfilled almost to the letter by Jesus. From his baptism he was endorsed by the heavenly voice, which Matthew, Mark and Luke all record. In his ministry he cares for the hurt and under-privileged and extends that role to the Gentiles, not just to his own nation. In doing this he links his servant-hood to his messianic introduction of the kingdom and teaches that kingship involves servanthood.

In the second Song (Isaiah 49:1–6), the Servant calls on the nations to listen. He has been called and named from his mother's womb, equipped silently for his coming task which will reach out beyond his own people to the whole Gentile world with a message of salvation, of light to those living in darkness.

Once again Jesus fits the template to a 't'. The second Song expands the first. Luke's Gospel (1:31–33) speaks of the angel's message to Mary in almost identical terms, as does Matthew's (1:20–21). In both accounts, the coming infant is named Yeshua, the deliverer, known in Greek as 'Jesus'. He is to be quietly trained for 30 years, brought up as the son of a small-town carpenter. Unlike the rigidly orthodox religious teachers of his day, he is willing to help those in need among the surrounding nations, whether a Roman soldier (Matthew 8:5–13) or a desperate Canaanite mother (Matthew 15:22–28). The chief difference between the two Songs is that Yahweh speaks in the first and the Servant speaks in the second. In both the task is the same.

The third Song (Isaiah 50:4–9), also spoken by the Servant, returns to his teaching role. Yahweh has taught and continues to teach him, but his message is essentially one of sustenance for those who are tired and in need. The theme changes at this point. The Servant's person and work are not respected. He is attacked physically, insulted and spat upon, his beard torn and his back flogged. Nevertheless, in spite of all the pain and provocation, he stands firm, knowing that he will be vindicated by Yahweh. Once more the fulfilment is more than evident in the passion of Jesus of Nazareth. In the high priest's court he is struck and spat upon (Matthew 26:67–68), then handed over to the Roman procurator, Pontius Pilate, who has him flogged by his soldiers. They too strike him and spit on him. In this third Song, the Servant becomes the 'Suffering Servant', as did Jesus on that terrible day in Jerusalem.

Before we consider the last of the Songs, we need to return to that pregnant scene in Caesarea Philippi (Matthew 16:13–20), which we noted as we looked at the development of the messianic idea earlier. Peter, suddenly imbued with certainty, declared, 'You are the Messiah, the Son of the living God' and was congratulated by Jesus for his insight, which had come not from his own wits but from Yahweh himself.

At that point we come to an amazing episode. Peter, having grasped the truth and doubtless feeling on top of the world, is appalled to hear Jesus launching into a fearful description of the fate awaiting him in the city of Jerusalem. This Messiah, instead of conquering the occupation forces of Caesar and reinstating the Davidic monarchy in his own person, now describes the suffering and execution which will be his lot at the hands of the leaders of his own nation. 'Impossible,' storms Peter. 'There's no way such a thing can happen' (Matthew 16:21–22). Then comes the terrible blow. First, Jesus uses the same words as those he had used when tempted in the desert by the Devil (Matthew 4:10): 'Clear off, Satan.' The word 'Satan' (both in Hebrew and Greek) means 'the opponent, the adversary'—in other words, the one who attempts to frustrate Yahweh's purposes. The shock to Peter's system must have been enormous. He had just grasped who Jesus really was, been congratulated, and, having attempted to prevent Jesus from a mad expectation of suffering and death, then found himself cast off as one trying to get in Yahweh's way!

Worse still, Jesus had called him 'Peter' (the little rock) and had spoken, in a pun, of building his church on the 'petra' (the great rock) of his confession of faith in Jesus as Messiah (16:18). Now, not only is he called 'Satan' but also a 'stumbling block' (the Greek is *skandalon*), which means the kind of stone over which the unwary can trip (16:23). In his first letter, written many years later, Peter links the words together (1 Peter 2:6, 8), so he clearly never forgot the awful warning that Jesus had given him. Even so, it was a very hard lesson for any of those early followers of Jesus to grasp that Messiah and Suffering Servant were one and the same person.

So we return, with this in our minds, to the fourth and last of Isaiah's Servant Songs (52:13—53:12). Here, in phrase after phrase, the Servant's agony is spelt out. Despised and rejected, a man of suffering, held of no account, a bearer of human sin who prayed for his persecutors, oppressed and afflicted, a silent sacrificial lamb, carrying human infirmity, with an appearance so marred as to be unrecognizable—all these phrases ring bell after bell as a description of the crucifixion of Jesus of Nazareth. Even in his death he is to be buried in the tomb of a rich man. On and on the account goes, with line after line fulfilled in the events surrounding the day at Calvary when Messiah, the crowned king on the throne of the cross, took on the awful task of the prophesied Suffering Servant and completed both roles at the same time and in the same place.

Jesus had indeed prophesied that he himself would be both Messiah and Suffering Servant, but he did not stop there. In that same prophecy he had concluded with the words 'and on the third day be raised'. Matthew, Mark and Luke all record these words but they clearly had the benefit of hindsight, writing as they did many years later. None of the followers of Jesus, it seems, had any serious expectation of any such thing. The few who remained with him at his death (mostly women) hastily laid him in the tomb provided by Joseph of Arimathea, a sympathetic member of the Sanhedrin. All four evangelists include this fact and couple it with the statement that the body was placed in linen wrappings and laid in a tomb sealed by a stone rolled across the entrance. John adds that Nicodemus joined them and placed 30 kilogrammes of spices within the wrappings. Then they went home.

The story of the resurrection, the empty tomb, and the dozen or more appearances of Jesus from the Sunday onwards are evidence that most Christians have accepted over the centuries since. In the mid-1960s, Archbishop Michael Ramsey put it more succinctly than anyone else, in a television interview with David Frost. 'No resurrection; no Christianity' were his words.

On that same Sunday, the first Easter Day, Luke (24:13–33) describes an extraordinary encounter between two followers of Jesus and a man whom they did not recognize, on the road between Jerusalem and the village of Emmaus, seven miles from the city. Together all three discussed the events that had led the two to hope that Jesus 'was the one to redeem Israel'—which is to say that they hoped that he was, indeed, Messiah. They added that there was a rumour going around that some woman had claimed that he had risen.

At that point the stranger chided them for their failure to grasp 'all that the prophets have declared. Was it not necessary', he added, 'that the Messiah should suffer these things and then enter into this glory?' He went on to spell out how such things were to be understood from 'Moses and all the prophets'.

Later that night, Jesus appeared to the eleven remaining disciples and some others, and repeated his explanation to them, opening their 'minds to understand the scriptures' and showing how it had been written long before 'that Messiah is to suffer and to rise from the dead'. Finally he alerted them to their task of proclaiming 'repentance and forgiveness of sins… to all nations, beginning from Jerusalem' since they were 'witnesses of these things' (Luke 24:36–48).

At last the realization that Messiah had to suffer began to sink in. A few days later, Peter preached to a crowd in the temple that 'God fulfilled what he had foretold through all the prophets, that his Messiah would suffer' (Acts 3:18).

Not long afterwards, the apostles appointed some assistants to help organize the infant Church's practical care, one of whom was Philip. One day he found himself helping an Ethiopian diplomat who was reading the Isaiah 'Suffering Servant' passage. The diplomat could not grasp what it was all about and Philip explained that it was Jesus who fulfilled the prophecy. The diplomat was baptized and returned home in his chariot, rejoicing.

Paul, also, did his utmost both in the synagogues of the Diaspora (Acts 13:2–5) and before King Agrippa II (great-grandson of King Herod the Great) to explain that 'Messiah must suffer, and that, by being the first to rise from the dead, he would proclaim light both to our people and to the Gentiles' (Acts 26:23).

The implications of this began to dawn on the apostles when the Sanhedrin had them flogged for preaching in the temple. Luke tells us (Acts 5:41) that 'they rejoiced that they were considered worthy to suffer dishonour for the sake of the name'.

Eventually, Peter, in his first letter, demonstrated that he had long since grasped the truth of the matter. Thirty years on from the embarrassing debacle at Caesarea Philippi, he used his understanding of the role of Jesus as the suffering Messiah to help and encourage Christians in north-western Turkey who were facing persecution for their faith. He had himself, he tells them, been 'a witness of the sufferings of Christ' (1 Peter 5:1) (that is to say, 'Messiah'), and from that position he was able to explain that they too must expect to suffer for their faith, which will test its genuineness as gold is tested in the fire (1:6–7). Messiah had suffered for them, thus leaving them an example to follow (2:21). He did so 'once and for all' (that is to say on one occasion only—the passage is not about the fact that he died 'for all'). By that one act he gave Christians a unique model showing that, however unjustly they may be treated, he had walked that same way, not abusing his persecutors or threatening them (2:23). Peter applies these words especially to slaves, who in the Roman world had no rights and could be whipped at their master's will. To accept this suffering, however unjust it might be if they had done nothing to deserve it, would bring them God's approval (2:20). They, like Jesus before them, must entrust themselves to God's ultimate judgment, which will be absolutely just. In so doing, their pains would be healed by the Messiah's wounds.

In accepting this, Christians would be helped (in John Goldingay's phrase) to understand that 'Jesus is the Servant par excellence'. He, as the Servant, was called to 'bring light to the nations'. Thus in sending his followers out into the Gentile world he was returning 'the servant calling to the people of God to whom it first belonged'. This is the task committed to all Christians, whatever the cost, and 'those who reckon to be members of the messianic people cannot escape its challenge to them'.[25]

Once more we see how the crucifixion is central to the whole divine purpose. The Messiah is nailed to his throne, where, in Pilate's words placed on the plaque above his head, he is seen as 'King of the Jews'. At that very moment the Servant-King bears the sin of the world, conscious of the spiritual agony of having been abandoned (Mark 15:34 together with Isaiah 53:5, 6, 10). So, in the utter darkness, he fights his lonely battle and completes the work that he alone could undertake. At last he cries out in triumph (John recalls it as a single Greek word, '*tetelestai*', which means 'I've done it'). The usual phrase, 'It is finished', is all too often read as a weary gasp of dying exhaustion. It is nothing of the sort. William Barclay, calling to mind Matthew's reference to Jesus having cried out 'with a loud voice' (27:50), says, 'Jesus died with a shout of triumph on his lips... he shouted for joy because the victory is won'.[26] Isaiah's Servant Songs reach their climax: 'Out of his anguish he shall see light; he shall find satisfaction' (53:11).

The most vivid passage in the New Testament, which teaches unambiguously that the cross was the place of victory, is to be found in Paul's letter to the Colossians (2:14–15). On the cross, he says, Jesus 'disarmed the cosmic powers and authorities and made a public spectacle of them, leading them as captives in his triumphal procession' (REB). To take the horror and degradation of crucifixion, a punishment that Roman law declined to inflict on any Roman citizen, which it regarded as only fitting for slaves and members of conquered tribes—to take that and stand it on its head, turning it into the victorious triumphal process of a Roman military conquering general is a stunning and exciting transposition.

And that's not all. Paul, as a theologically trained rabbi, was well aware that Deuteronomy lays a curse on anyone crucified. He reminds the Galatians that 'cursed is everyone who hangs on a tree' (3:13). Yet, through his triumphant victory, Jesus drew the sting from the curse by 'becoming a curse for us', and thus the tree, symbol of unsanctified death and judgment, became, at the suffering Messiah's hands, the Tree of Life.

THE BRANCH OF PRIESTHOOD: JESUS THE HIGH PRIEST

It wasn't too difficult for the early Christians to understand Jesus as Messiah. Before long he was being called 'Jesus Christ', which means 'the anointed saviour' and his teaching and signs were clearly understood as the fulfilment of Old Testament prophetic expectation. So far, so good.

It took a little longer for them to make the connection between a royal king in the Davidic line and the
Suffering Servant of the prophet Isaiah's words. But they
got there soon after the resurrection of Jesus. As we have
seen, the amazing idea that there could be a suffering
Messiah, a king on a cross, a cursed blasphemer, being
the focus of God's blessing as the saviour of the world
was in complete conflict with the tradition in which any
Jewish man grew up. But they got there.

The third problem was not so easily soluble. As
we have seen, the 'covenant tree' had three branches.
We have considered two but, with one to go, the
connection between Jesus and priesthood was almost
impossible to maintain. Aaron's line was the priestly line
and there was no evident connection with Jesus, whose
genealogy, whether in the Matthean or Lucan versions,
shows him to have descended from Judah, through
David. Aaron descended from Levi, Judah's elder
brother. How, then, could there possibly be any direct
link for Jesus with the priestly line? Indeed, the author
of the letter to the Hebrews, who set himself the task
of creating the priestly connection for Jesus, openly
acknowledged (7:13–14) that Jesus was not of the
priestly line but rather that of Judah. That, he says, 'is
evident' (7:14). So, the author has a job on his hands.
How can any connection be established?

As we saw earlier, the inner area of the temple had
two connected rooms. The first, called the 'Holy Place',
led into the inner sanctuary, the 'Holy of Holies'. This
inner room was a perfect cube, representing God's
presence. It was hidden behind a curtain ('the veil') and

only the high priest was permitted to enter it once a year on *Yom Kippur*, the day of atonement. The curtain, always closed across the entrance, was a powerful symbol of exclusion. None but the high priest, on his annual incursion to seek mercy and forgiveness for himself and the nation, could expect or claim direct access to Yahweh, utterly holy divinity as he was. The curtain kept humanity, even Jewish humanity, firmly in its place—outside the presence chamber and needing a mediator in the person of the high priest and the sacrifice whose blood he carried with him. Every Jew knew the rules.

Matthew's Gospel, written by and for people of that nation, made an extraordinary assertion. It was repeated in briefer form by both Mark and Luke, writing for Romans and Greeks, and it referred to that very curtain. 'At that moment,' said Matthew, speaking of Messiah's last breath, 'the curtain of the temple was torn in two, from top to bottom'. This phenomenon was accompanied, he added, by an earthquake—'the earth shook' (27:51).

'Up to this time,' says William Barclay, 'God had been hidden and remote, and no man knew what he was like.' Now, he adds, 'the way to the presence of God once barred to all men is now opened to all'.[27] R.T. France agrees and goes on to point out that 'top to bottom' shows 'that this was the work not of man but of God'.[28]

Jesus, through this symbol, had done more than the high priest could ever do. He had opened up the way, carrying the blood of his own sacrifice, and done it once and for all so that it could never, and would never, be repeated. No longer was an annual atonement, available only to the nation, necessary. From now onwards, the way into God's living presence was opened, and not just symbolically.

Moreover, in the week before his crucifixion, Jesus had warned his hearers in the temple that this great building in all its splendour would 'be thrown down' and 'not one stone will be left here upon another' (Matthew 24:2). The words, once more, are used also by Mark and Luke. Throughout his trial before the Sanhedrin, these words of prophecy were twisted into the assertion that he had said that he would himself 'destroy the temple of God' (Matthew 26:61).

The prophecy came true 40 years later when, following a revolt by the Jewish people against the Romans, Caesar's soldiers destroyed it, never to be rebuilt. It had been completed only six years earlier, having been over 80 years in its building, begun by King Herod the Great in 19BC. The high priesthood and Sanhedrin were abolished. Another revolt took place in AD132 and the emperor Hadrian ordered Jerusalem to be flattened and the Jewish people barred from what was left.

Jesus, then, sensed that his work on the cross and his coming ascension were, in theological terms, the kiss of death for the temple and its rituals. He did not, however, say much to his disciples about this aspect of his ministry and they, initially, do not seem to have drawn such a conclusion. Indeed, they launched their preaching ministry in the temple (Acts 3) and the whole group of disciples spent a great deal of their time there (Acts 2:46). Paul, in later years, on trial before Festus the procurator, could say with conviction that he had 'in no way committed an offence… against the temple' (Acts 25:8). Virtually the only recorded remark that could be construed as even vaguely critical of the temple was made by Stephen, at the climax of his defence before the Sanhedrin. Speaking of God, he declared that it was Solomon 'who built a house for him. Yet,' he added, 'the Most High does not dwell in houses made by human hands' (Acts 7:47–48). Seconds later, having insulted his hearers, he was dragged out of Jerusalem and stoned to death.

Not until an unknown Christian wrote a letter to some Jewish people (the letter to the Hebrews) did the matter of the temple, the priesthood and the sacrificial system came to the fore. It has been said that this letter 'is in many respects the riddle of the New Testament'.[29] No one knows for sure who wrote it, and when. It was probably written in Rome and most probably to Christian Jews. The likely date is the late 60s but this is believed largely because the letter contains no reference to the destruction of the temple in AD70 (which would have added considerable weight to the author's case). We cannot be sure of date, place or author and it was one of the last documents to be generally accepted into the canon of the New Testament. The fact that Clement of Rome (c. AD95) seemed to quote from it added strength to the conviction that it was both early and authentic.

What is unique and important about this letter? As we have already noted, Jesus did not come from the tribe of Levi (the priestly tribe) and, therefore, on the face of it, while fulfilling both the messianic and prophetic roles of anointed Suffering Servant, he seemed an unlikely candidate to be the 'great high priest'.

Two ideas dominate the letter, which we must consider before we look at the immediate question of Jesus' qualification for the role of priesthood. The author repeatedly uses the word 'better' in order to establish the comparison between the Christian faith and Judaism. The word he uses carries the sense of 'more excellent' or 'superior'. Jesus is 'superior' to the angels since he is the 'heir of all things', being 'the exact imprint of God's very being' (Hebrews 1:2–3). He it is who offers 'a better hope, through which we approach God' (7:19) and guarantees a more excellent 'covenant' (7:22). Moreover, this 'better covenant' is based on 'better promises' (8:6) and effected by 'better sacrifices' than those of animals in the temple (9:23). In consequence, despite all their sufferings, the Christian believers enjoy a 'better and more lasting' inheritance (10:34).

Why was this stress on the 'better' necessary? The letter shows only too clearly that some of its readers were in danger of slipping back into the ritual of the temple and its sacrificial system (6:4–12) in order to fill the gap that the life and worship of the Church left unfilled. As Guthrie puts it, Christians 'had no altar, no priests, no sacrifices' and 'no parallel to the ritual trappings to which they had been accustomed'.[30] A similar charge was often levelled by the pagan world, which called the Christians 'atheists' because of their lack of idols.[31]

The author, then, has to demonstrate that, in Jesus, things are not less, but more, excellent. This extends even to Jesus' relationship to Moses, the most revered figure in Jewish history. Jesus, quite simply, 'is worthy of more glory' (3:3).

What about the second dominant idea in the letter to the Hebrews? The first hundred words make it absolutely plain. There is, bluntly, a finality about Jesus, his nature and his work, that is absolutely unique: whereas 'God spoke to our ancestors in many and various ways by the prophets... in these last days he has spoken to us by a Son' (1:1–2). The tenses used contrast the past developing revelation with the new and decisive proclamation by Jesus. In the same way, the fact of his 'purification for sins' (1:3) is expressed through a completed action tense (aorist). In short, what Jesus said and what he did was to be the last word on the matter of human salvation. It was, on the cross, achieved, and by his further act of sitting down at the 'right hand of the Majesty on high' (also the aorist tense) it was finally completed. His heavenly role involved no further offering or presentation of the unique sacrifice. Seated, he 'intercedes' on behalf of his faithful followers (7:25). Paul, in his letter to the Romans, uses the same rare verb (Romans 8:27, 34). Thus, his sacrificial ministry completed for eternity, Jesus brings the needs of his people into the heavenly presence chamber, the actual 'holy of holies' (and not, like the historic high priest, into a symbolic secret room, in a action needing annual repetition on the Day of Atonement). The ripping down of the curtain spoke volumes about the consequences of his cry from the cross—'It is completed'.

With this background, then, the author of the Hebrews letter begins his explanation of the way in which Jesus was the unique high priest who wound up for ever the old ritual system of the temple sacrifices, and especially that of the Day of Atonement entry into the Holy of Holies. He sets it all out in four chapters (7—10).

He begins his argument by admitting, without embarrassment, that 'it is evident that our Lord was descended from Judah, and in connection with that tribe Moses said nothing about priests' (7:14). So he turns to the strange, shadowy person of Melchizedek, mentioned only twice in the Old Testament.

Shortly before God made his covenant promise to Abraham, the patriarch met a man described as 'priest of God Most High'. He is introduced to us as 'King Melchizedek of Salem' (which actually means 'king of righteousness and king of peace'). Most commentators think that 'Salem' was a shortened form of 'Jerusalem'. Melchizedek blessed Abraham, who gave him ten per cent of the booty he had recently collected after a battle (Genesis 14:18–20). The only other Melchizedek reference in the Old Testament is in Psalm 110 which, while its original meaning remains a matter of dispute, is the most quoted, or alluded to, passage from the Old Testament mentioned in the New Testament. Peter sees it as a messianic reference to Jesus (Acts 2:34), as does Paul (1 Corinthians 15:25; Colossians 3:1). In both Matthew's and Mark's Gospels, Jesus is said to have used the same Psalm in its messianic sense. The author of the Hebrews letter uses it many times (1:3, 13; 5:6; 6:20 and in chapters 7—10). It became a crucial passage in the early Church's understanding of Christ's high priesthood.

Our author's thesis is that, first, Melchizedek was superior to Abraham; and since Levi and his descendants were 'in the loins' of Abraham (Levi was Abraham's great-grandson) they were evidently inferior to Melchizedek, who accepted the tithe of the booty from Abraham and blessed him (Hebrews 7:4–10). Second, since Jesus is Messiah and therefore, following Psalm 110's messianic prophecy, he is 'a priest for ever according to the order of Melchizedek' (Psalm 110:4), that makes his priesthood superior to, and of a different order from, that of the family of Levi and Aaron, its first recognized high priest.[32] Third, whereas the historic priests were subject to death, Jesus 'continues for ever' and, being 'holy, blameless, undefiled, separated from sinners', he has been 'exalted above the heavens' (7:24, 26). Unlike all the other high priests 'once for all… he offered himself' (7:27) and is thus 'the mediator of a better covenant' since 'he entered once for all into the Holy Place, not with the blood of goats and calves, but with his own blood, thus obtaining eternal redemption' (8:6; 9:12). Unlike the high priest, Jesus 'did not enter a sanctuary made by human hands, a mere copy of the true one, but he entered into heaven itself' (9:24). There is therefore 'no longer any offering for sin' (10:18). To those who accept and believe this comes 'confidence to enter the sanctuary by the blood of Jesus… in full assurance of faith' (10:19, 22).

So the powerful imagery of our tree's three branches comes together at the cross. As we have seen, the king gets his throne, and it is the cross. The Servant fulfils his calling to be despised and rejected as he wears his crown of thorns on the cross. Finally the high priest offers himself, a sinless sacrifice, on the altar of the cross. Thus the letter to the Hebrews recognizes that 'we have an altar' (13:10), just as we have a high priest and a perfect sacrifice. All find their focus at Calvary where 'Christ bore our sins', in William Tyndale's translation of 1 Peter 2:24, 'on the tree'.

The Bible begins and ends with a tree—it is the same tree and it is called 'the tree of life'. Two other great symbolic trees play their part. The tree of the knowledge of good and evil is in Eden and the man and the woman disobediently pillage it and pay the price. The other tree tells us of a man who pays another price. His name is Jesus and that tree was erected on the hill called Golgotha. He was nailed to that tree as prophet, priest and king, and from that altar-throne he sent out a people with good news for the world. The covenant promise that had been made to Abraham was now theirs and they had a massive task to fulfil. 'Go,' he commanded them, 'and make disciples of all nations… And remember, I am with you always' (Matthew 28:19–20).

And he has been.

BEARING FRUIT

The imagery of the fruit-bearing tree is one that is widely used in the New Testament. All four Gospel authors mention it as part of the teaching of Jesus. Paul uses it in writing to six of his recipients. So does James, and so does the author of the letter to the Hebrews. Lastly, in the book of Revelation (22:2) the tree of life itself bears fresh fruit every month of the year and its leaves heal the nations. This last-mentioned idea has its origins in the prophecy of Ezekiel (47:12) where an almost identical phrase is used. William Barclay records a similar phrase from rabbinic tradition. 'In the age to come,' says one of them, 'God will create trees which will produce fruit in any month and the man who eats from them will be healed'.[33]

In his teaching, Jesus contrasts the existence and produce of good and bad trees. 'Every good tree,' he says, 'bears good fruit, but the bad tree bears bad fruit'. The consequence, he concludes, is that bad trees are cut down and thrown into the fire (Matthew 7:17–19). Not surprisingly, he has certain people in mind in saying this and, in reintroducing the tree and fruit theme (Matthew 12:33–34), he identifies the hostile Pharisees, who accuse him of healing and exorcising by the power of Beelzebub, prince of demons.

Throughout much of the New Testament, the tension between traditionalist and Christian Jews simmers. Initially it wasn't 'Christians vs. Jews', since almost all the followers of Jesus were themselves from the Jewish nation and were proud to be so. In due course, Paul, 'a Pharisee, a son of Pharisees' as he described himself (Acts 23:6), who remained deeply conscious, with gratitude, of his Israelite ancestry, was quite unwilling to believe that God had rejected his ancient people (Romans 11:1–2). He was, nevertheless, frequently attacked and vilified by local and national leaders from the synagogues and the Sanhedrin. Having himself been present at the stoning of Stephen, of which he approved (Acts 7:58—8:1), he could have had little doubt about the passionate opposition to Jesus and his disciples within some parts of the Jewish community both in Jerusalem and other parts of the Roman empire.

By the end of the first century, it seems possible that a majority of Christians were no longer from Jewish, but rather from Gentile, families. Certainly this was true by AD150. Two factors would then come into play. First, these Gentiles would from childhood have inherited the widespread suspicion of most things Jewish. Second, as Christians, they would have been more than aware that Jesus, though himself a Jew, had faced persecution from the leaders of his nation during his lifetime, and that his followers had been, or were thought to have been, the victims of Jewish hostility, either directly or through pressure brought to bear on the Gentile authorities to punish Christians. Thus the seeds of anti-Semitism were sown and the terrible story of Christian hostility towards the Jewish people began its long and lethal development. Whatever the initial provocation caused by Jewish persecution in the earliest days of the Church, the hatred, bitterness, distrust and ultimate attempt at genocide could never have been justified by anything that Jesus had taught. 'Love your enemies' is hardly a recipe for anti-Semitic persecution.

Even at the end of the 20th century, books still appeared from within the Jewish community (and the more liberal parts of it at that) which, while welcoming the criticisms of the Old Testament prophets, attacked Jesus and the apostles for saying many of the same things.[34] Moreover, the writers do not seem to be aware how their ancestors behaved towards the first Christians, behaviour that must carry some responsibility for the awful history of anti-Semitism that resulted. Undoubtedly Jewish–Christian relationships would be greatly improved if both sides (and not just one) were to admit to some guilt over the past two thousand years. Sadly, even to say that seems to be regarded as a form of anti-Semitism.

Most ancient of all the hostile criticisms was the one that Paul attempted to counter in his letters to the Galatians and Romans. We can reasonably assume (though it isn't explicitly stated) that he had been faced with the argument that what he was doing was to found a new religion which was quite distinct from Judaism and the Old Testament. Even today, most Jewish people (and especially their leaders) deny that there can be any such animal as a Jewish Christian. They agree that you can be an atheist Jew, a Communist Jew, an immoral Jew, indeed almost any kind of Jew, but you cannot be a Jew and a Christian. Christians who are born Jews (Messianic Jews is their description of themselves) are, not surprisingly, hurt when their deeply held conviction that as good Jews they have accepted Jesus as the promised Messiah is rejected.

Paul found such an attitude entirely unacceptable. To him God's covenant with Abraham was eternal (Genesis 17:7) and he sets out, briefly in Galatians and in more detail in Romans, to maintain that all Christians, whatever their ethnic origin, are Abraham's offspring. He actually calls us all, male or female, 'Abraham's sperm' (Galatians 3:29)!

His brief argument in his Galatians letter (3:6–9) is that, since 'Abraham believed God and it was reckoned to him as righteousness' (cf. Genesis 15:6) then in the same way, 'those who believe are the descendants of Abraham' since God has already promised that 'all the Gentiles shall be blessed in you'. Thus, 'those who believe are blessed with Abraham who believed'.

Paul expands this idea in his Roman letter (4:1–25). Since Christians are not 'justified by works', neither was Abraham. Again he quotes Genesis 15:6 that 'Abraham believed God', and goes on to point out that this was before Abraham had accepted circumcision. That circumcision, he argued, was 'a seal of the righteousness that he had by faith while he was still uncircumcised'. In this way he was ancestor both of the circumcised and the uncircumcised, provided that both believed in the covenant promise. The promise, Paul continues, 'did not come... through the law but through the righteousness of faith'. In this way the promise rests on

God's grace, and Abraham did not waver 'but grew strong in his faith'. In short, concludes Paul, righteousness 'will be reckoned to us who believe'. Abraham's belief was in a promise that, despite having no son and being, with his wife, well beyond normal parental age, God would indeed make him 'the father of many nations'. Our belief is in the same God 'who raised Jesus from the dead'.

Thus, Jew or Gentile, we will be justified on the ground of faith. But, in a later chapter (Romans 9:6–8), Paul distinguishes between literal and spiritual descent. 'Not all Israelites', he says, 'truly belong to Israel, and not all of Abraham's children are his true descendants'. Thus 'it is not the children of the flesh who are the children of God, but the children of the promise'. These, he concludes, 'are counted as descendants'.

The covenant that matters, then, is the eternal covenant made by God with Abraham which has as its true descendants those who trust in God and his promises. They may be Jews, they may be Gentiles, but essentially they are trusting believers, looking to see God's promise fulfilled as they bring blessing upon the world. They are the community of faith.

Having said that, Paul returns to the tree theme. In Romans 11:17–24, he illustrates the Jew–Gentile relationship by the example of an olive tree. Gentile Christians, he suggests, are like wild olive branches that have been grafted into the true olive tree, which had lost some of its branches when they broke off. In that situation, some humility is needed. The Gentiles are not the original branches, so, glad as they are to have been grafted in, they must not make it a matter for pride. The right attitude must be one of awe that God should, in his mercy, have grafted them into his tree. The broken branches were lost through unbelief, in contrast to the newly grafted ones who are there through faith. But there is a warning. Grafted they may have been, but they also can be pruned away if they forget God's mercy. It could even be that if the original branches, the unbelieving Jews, recover a true belief, they too can be grafted back into the tree. That is Paul's hope, for God still loves them.

Now where does all this get us? Surely it enables us to see that the Christian Church is not some Johnny-come-lately which suddenly arrived on the scene on the day of Pentecost. To declare piously that Pentecost is the birthday of the Church is to misconceive the whole history of God's eternal promise. It remains for ever the same promise, for God has called into being a community of faith. That community is made up of Abraham's descendants-by-faith whose ultimate destiny is the new heaven and the new earth, where there is no temple sanctuary in God's holy city, Jerusalem, since God himself and the Lamb are its focus, its light and its lamp (Revelation 21:22–23). Its throne is centred on God and the Lamb, and living water flows from it. The Lamb is, of course, Jesus and he invites those who are faithful to eat from the tree of life in God's garden paradise (Revelation 2:7). The imagery is stunning, vivid, and speaks of total satisfaction in God's very presence, to which the Bride (the holy city) and the Holy Spirit say 'Come!' There they will drink of the water of life.

A PROMISE FULFILLED

That first generation of Christians had among them a small group of leaders who grasped one vital matter. What they had learned from Jesus was that he was not some totally new phenomenon but rather the fulfilment of the saving promise of God made 1500 or more years earlier to Abraham. From the very nature of God had come the expression of his intention to build a community founded on one man whom he had chosen, the nomad Abram with whom he had made a covenant which would never be withdrawn. Expressing the truth of that promise, as we have seen, a trio of key developments came into being—a priesthood, a kingdom and a prophetic response. All looked forward to the time of a priestly, suffering Messiah. In Jesus, God had come to his community to save them, and with the return of Messiah to the heavenly throne, the same reality, no longer visible or tangible, had come among them in a new way, the true Spirit of God.

These same Christian leaders and their associates set out, in teaching, preaching and writing, to encourage their small but growing community to see that the whole group had now been called to be a suffering, royal priesthood, entrusted with the task of bringing the good news of a saviour to Jerusalem, Judea, and the ends of the earth. In taking on this responsibility, they were, in fact, doing no more than completing the work that God had long ago given to Abraham. In terms of the tree analogy that we have been using, the covenant and its three branches found a single focus in one man on a cross and then opened up into the transformed community that he had sent into the whole world. They were thus to be a messianic royal people, a suffering and prophetic people, and a priestly people offering their lives, their praise and their worship as, in Paul's words, 'a living sacrifice, holy and acceptable to God' (Romans 12:1). This group was, in a similar description provided by Peter, 'a chosen race, a royal priesthood, a holy nation, God's own people' who had been called 'out of darkness into his marvellous light' (1 Peter 2:9).

Despite this, a serious question must have puzzled the Christians. How were they to be related to the people of the covenant made with Moses? When the Jewish nation left Egypt and set out for Mount Sinai and the promised land, God had made a covenant with them. It had been sealed in blood, splashed upon all of them. According to the book of Exodus (24:7–8), Moses took the book of the covenant and read it in the hearing of the people and they said, 'All that the Lord has spoken we will do, and we will be obedient.' At that point 'Moses took the blood and dashed it on the people', saying, 'See the blood of the covenant that the Lord has made with you in accordance with all these words.'

The covenant with Noah, that there would never again be a universal flood, was timeless. So too was the covenant with Abraham. The covenant with David promised that one of his descendants would always be on the throne, but it had a qualification: if they disobeyed, it would not stand. In due course it was interpreted as a promise of the coming Messiah.

What, then, of the covenant with Israel and its sacrificial system, centred on the temple and the 'Holy of Holies'? This was not described in Exodus as an 'eternal' covenant, and the letter to the Hebrews speaks of it in no uncertain terms as 'obsolete' and ready to 'disappear' (8:13). Thus, says the writer, 'Jesus has now obtained a more excellent ministry' for 'he is the mediator of a better covenant, which has been enacted through better promises' (8:6). The consequence is that Jesus 'abolishes the first in order to establish the second' (10:9). By 'the first', the writer clearly means the covenant made at Sinai. By 'the second', he means... well, what does he mean?

So we come to our final two, related, covenants. The prophet Jeremiah declares, at the time of the exile to Babylon, that the 'days are surely coming, says the Lord, when I will make a new covenant'. But this one will be radically different. 'It will not,' he states, 'be like the covenant that I made... when I took them by the hand to bring them out of the land of Egypt—a covenant that they broke.' In its place, by the new covenant, says God, 'I will put my law within them and I will write it on their hearts' (Jeremiah 31:31–33).

When did this new covenant commence? Surely on the night before the crucifixion of Jesus when he took bread and wine and described the latter as 'the new covenant in my blood'. The covenant in blood was a powerful link, and yet a discontinuity, with the Mosaic act at Sinai which Exodus described as 'the blood of the covenant'. Having taken the wine with these words, Jesus went on to command his disciples to eat and drink, from then onwards, 'in remembrance of me', thus proclaiming his death until his return (1 Corinthians 11:25–26). Moreover, this 'new covenant in my blood' is 'poured out for many for the forgiveness of sins' (Luke 22:20; Matthew 26:28). The bread and wine were indeed the powerful signs of the sacrificed flesh and blood which would, on the next day, be the actual enactment of the new covenant provided by Jesus.

The better covenant, provided by the better mediator, offered better promises, and 'the new covenant in my blood' was to be recalled by the followers of Jesus whenever they gathered to give him thanks. Bread and wine would indeed be 'his body and his blood' for Christians the world over.

So the Christian community is grounded on two covenants—the first, made by God to Abraham and all who, like him, believe that God keeps his promises; and the second, made by Jesus to his disciples, which speaks powerfully of the cross on which God's promise was fulfilled.

THE NEW PEOPLE: GOD'S CHURCH

The Greek word for 'church' is *ecclesia*, and it appears 107 times in the New Testament. Interestingly, only

three of these mentions are in the Gospels. (Although all of those are by Jesus, only once does he use the word in relation to the 'people of God' in the theological sense, and that is on the pivotal occasion when Peter acknowledged his Messiahship at Caesarea Philippi.) The vast majority of these mentions—over 80—are in the writings of Paul. *'Ecclesia'* means 'those called out' and it captures perfectly the 'community of Abraham', called out to be the people of the promise.

Many metaphors are also used to stress particular aspects of that community. Among others are body, bride, fellowship, building, royal priesthood, living temple, flock, holy nation, chosen race, and God's own people.

One of the most interesting and important aspects of the *ecclesia* is that, from Abraham's time onwards, it is a people to whom a promise is offered. It does not begin with a 'doctrinal basis', although, due to many disagreements in and on the edge of the community, a need for definition became essential in due course. Thus the Church worked out 'creeds', based on biblical teaching, though sometimes using non-biblical words to describe especial subtleties, not least those relating to the Greek mind and culture of early Gentile Christians. Perhaps the most pithy and instructive phrase was used to describe the essential nature of the *ecclesia*. It was, as we say in the Nicene Creed, 'one, holy, catholic and apostolic' and, despite disputes and divisions, these four adjectives became the most accepted definition of the community's nature for most of its history.

Why those four? Two of them are directly biblical but

two come from a slightly later period. 'Catholic' is first found in the letter of Ignatius, bishop of Antioch, to Smyrna, written somewhere within the period AD100–115. Ignatius wrote a series of letters to various churches while being taken in chains to Rome, there to be martyred. He and a collection of later writers also stressed the 'apostolic' teaching as the one guarantee of authenticity. Jesus stressed the need for 'one' church and the word 'holy' is widely used in the letters of Peter and Paul to describe the Christian community.

It can hardly be accidental, then, that the *ecclesia* is itself a credal doctrine. In that respect it is a 'first level' concept. Only in some of the independent Protestant groups that arose during and after the 16th-century Reformation was it reduced to 'second level', and that concept became widespread among 'inter-denomin-ational' bodies from the mid-19th century onwards. It is therefore not surprising that it was from such denominations and groups, especially in the United States, that there arose a totally new concept of 'church' which has, by the present day, led to the development worldwide of some 25,000 different 'denominations'. These groups usually begin either from splits and schisms, often focused on a strong personality, and claiming that their 'basis of faith' is truly authentic.

So there are two polarized concepts. Are Christians 'a community chosen to enshrine and proclaim a truth' or, conversely, 'a truth enclustered by a chosen com-munity?' At first sight this may seem to be splitting hairs, but a few minutes' consideration opens up the huge divide that has historically resulted from the distinction. Neither concept would want to minimize the doctrinal importance of the content of Christian belief, but the former view (broadly summed up as 'catholicity') has largely managed to hold its adherents together, despite strong internal disagreements, whereas the latter (broadly categorized as 'evangelicalism') has a long history of divisions throughout virtually every century of its existence.

The *ecclesia* is to be 'one' because it rests in Christ, who is the 'head' of the 'body'. It must be 'holy' since that is the very title given to the whole community of Christ's followers in the New Testament—a 'set apart' people called to be his disciples. Then it must be 'catholic' because it is universal in its scope but not sectarian in character. (Both aspects of catholicity were vital, not just one or the other.) Lastly, it is to be 'apostolic' since it is the apostles' teaching and example that most closely link it to Jesus himself. They were the ones who knew him best and who could, therefore, pass on his most authentic word. Finally, within this Church, 'wheat and weeds' grow together as they do in Christ's parable of the kingdom until the ultimate harvest. Thus, it is called to perfection but he alone has the authority to sort one from the other.

The mid-point of this disjunction can probably be seen in the Church of England among evangelicals. They have retained the classic marks of 'catholicity'— namely the three creeds; the threefold ministry of bishops, priests, and deacons; and the two sacraments of baptism and holy communion. Side by side with these has gone a stress on the need for strong personal conviction and experience, grounded in specific theologies of the authority of scripture, of justification by faith, of a preaching tradition, and a degree of suspicion of episcopal leadership coupled with the reality of a conversion experience. For most of the past five hundred years, they have had an uneasy relationship with the formal structure and leadership of the church. Correct doctrinal definition has usually been the governing issue.

In the past 150 years, they have gone through periods when their sympathies have been more with other evangelicals outside the Church of England than with their fellow Anglicans. The reason for this is precisely because they have constantly been tempted to put the doctrine of the Church on to 'second level' rather than recognizing that its place in the Nicene Creed puts it firmly on to 'first level'. The consequence has been that many (especially lay) evangelicals move from denomination to denomination depending largely on the style and preaching of local faith communities and not on their ecclesiological doctrine.

We must examine this situation more carefully if we are to accept that the Abrahamic covenant is vital to an integrating theology of salvation, for, ironically, it is among evangelical Anglicans that the covenant concept has had its strongest advocates. At the beginning of the new millennium, evangelicals within the Church of England have been facing a crisis in their understanding of the doctrine of the Church, commonly called 'ecclesiology', and this is having a divisive effective on many of the practical consequences as regards the life of the Church of England and the reaction of evangelicals to it.

On the one hand, the historical position is held by some who, following Reformers such as Jewel, Whitgift and Hooker, believe that the Church of England has, until the last 30 years, perceived itself to be the catholic church of the land—a description that is not synonymous with 'universal' but that set it over against both Roman Catholicism on the one hand and nonconformity on the other.

On this view, the Church is rooted in the divine covenant with Abraham, continuing through the patristic period and throughout Christian history with a developing doctrine of threefold ministry which is consonant with the New Testament, and the norm is the 'one, holy, catholic and apostolic church'. Doctrine is essential, but it is not the governing issue.

From such a position of ecclesiological clarity, dialogue, fellowship and much mutual mission is possible both within and outside the Church of England between those of different traditions and denominations and a strong doctrinal basis can be adopted. A recent modification had seen the Church of England recognize reality by locating the Church of England as 'a part of the one, holy, catholic, and apostolic church',[35] a definition in which other 'parts' are not defined as included or excluded. On this view 'Anglican' is the noun and Evangelical the adjective.

An alternative view has developed throughout the last 100 years, stemming from the founding of the Evangelical Alliance and the Keswick convention, in which the test of a church's orthodoxy is largely governed by its theological attitude towards scripture and justification by grace through faith.

On this view, the essential element is not ecclesial continuity but a specific doctrinal formula in which 'Evangelical' is the noun and 'Anglican' no more than a qualifying adjective. This view treats the doctrine of the Church as secondary and, coming from an inter-denominational milieu, does not regard any Christian grouping as 'un-catholic' but places much less significance on the historical development of the three-fold ministry or the growth of a diocesan or provincial structure since the early centuries of the Church.

One consequence of this view is the perception of the Anglican church as 'provisional' and open to radical reshaping both internally and in its relationship with churches, not only of an episcopal or connectional kind, but even with independent churches, both post-Reformation and more recent in origin.

From these two 'shorthand' descriptions of currently held ecclesiologies among evangelicals within the Church of England come diverging responses to the ongoing life of the national church and to the other Christian groups, some at least of which have sectarian elements within their ethos and tradition.

Thus, some are more critical of her fundamental shape and structure, while others remain wedded to these, while being open to more limited areas of reform. Some see weakness in the elements of catholicity of structure and ministry; others wish strongly to affirm them. Critique and affirmation are difficult to hold together, but evangelicals in the past have managed this. The biblical clarity and spiritual generosity of evangelical leaders such as Charles Simeon and Norman Anderson, to name but two, remain as models for today.

It is clear from all of this that 'covenant theology' has major implications for the future of the Church. It affects the very nature of the Church and the relationships that exist between Christians of varying traditions. Those Christians who, for whatever reason, see little importance attaching to the promise made to Abraham and the sense of community continuity that stems from it do not perceive the Christian Church to be the same kind of animal as those who look back to Abraham as their spiritual founder under God. So we must ask, as Gareth Bennett did in his controversial Crockford Preface of 1987, 'Is the ecclesiology worked out by Jewel, Hooker and their successors, in the formative years of Anglican self-definition, understood, accepted and wanted today?'[36] And what was that ecclesiology? It was the conviction, as Jewel put it in his *Apology* (1562) that 'we have not departed from the primitive church, from the apostles, and from Christ' but rather we have 'returned to the apostles and the old catholic fathers'.[37] They, as we have seen, knew themselves to be (as Paul said) followers of Abraham, 'the ancestor of all who believe'.

Virtually every new Christian grouping since has tried to create 'a New Testament church' (as if it were possible to ditch two millennia overnight and start afresh tomorrow morning). That is what happens when the understanding of God's eternal covenant with

Abraham is misconceived as being the 'old' covenant rendered obsolete by Jesus.

Countless Christians across the world do not see themselves as part of the 'catholicity' tradition of the Abrahamic covenant. They are heirs of the idea that you can start a new church at will and there are, today, some 25,000 such 'churches'. Not a few of them reject those of us who stand in the Abraham tradition as not being genuine Christians.

How, then, should we respond? First, by standing firm in the conviction that we are not at liberty to discard the eternal covenant or regard it as a peripheral idea. It is deeply rooted not only in the Bible but also in the Nicene and Apostles' creeds. It affects the very nature of Christ's Church. We cannot spinelessly capitulate on this matter.

But secondly, we must accept that those who reject the Abraham tradition do not do so out of some wish to be unbiblical. They believe that they are Christians and seek to follow Christ as their Lord and Saviour. So we must not forget the awful warnings of the past when Christians burnt and disembowelled each other because of their certainty that they alone were the purveyors of the truth, the whole truth, and nothing but the truth. These awful warnings must alert us to our Christian calling to 'love one another' as Christ's brothers and sisters who, in Paul's words, are to 'speak the truth in love' and so 'grow up', being 'no longer children' (Ephesians 4:14, 15).

THE NEW SIGNS: BAPTISM AND COMMUNION

Human life, in its usual sense, begins with birth and can only last while there is genuine nourishment. The former is a unique experience but the latter is an ongoing, daily necessity. So it is with the Christian community: the two gospel sacraments, ordained by Jesus himself, lie at the very heart of the Christian community and always have done. Moreover, the Church has never been willing to consider separating the inner spiritual experiences that they demonstrate from the sacramental acts themselves. Bishop Stephen Neill was undoubtedly right when he said that 'non-sacramental Christianity… is an invention of the rationalistic nineteenth century: it has little to do with the Christianity of the New Testament and cannot be made to square with it'.

From the time of the Last Supper, Christians have 'done this' in remembrance of Jesus. This 'Eucharist' (which means a 'thanksgiving') was to be celebrated 'in remembrance of me', and at various points in the New Testament it is explicitly mentioned, sometimes simply as 'breaking bread' and at other times as 'the Lord's Supper'.

It was inaugurated by Jesus and specifically associated with the Passover meal. Taking bread and wine, he gave it to his disciples in the upper room chosen for the purpose and described the wine as 'the new covenant in my blood'. Perhaps surprisingly, in the light of the way in which he has come to be linked as 'a priest for ever after the order of Melchizedek', neither Jesus nor his disciples made any reference to the strange mention in Genesis 14:18 of the mysterious King Melchizedek's having 'brought out bread and wine' to set before Abraham. Needless to say, in the Christian era, this inexplicable reference was much mentioned, but never in the New Testament. Whatever the reason, the author of the letter to Hebrews clearly didn't want to raise the subject and, in the light of the well-meaning but far-fetched glosses later produced by Clement of Alexandria and Cyprian (in the third century), we are probably wise not to attempt to develop the idea.

The use, then, by Jesus of the word 'covenant' is the only one recorded in the Gospels and it obviously looks back to the covenant made by Yahweh with Moses and the Jewish people at Sinai. In that sense, Jesus is the new Moses, splashing the blood upon his compatriots. What we never get is any attempt to link Jesus and his 'new' covenant with the eternal covenant made by God with Abraham. Eucharistic language is closely linked with blood sacrifice, the sacrifices in the temple, and these Jesus clearly fulfilled and renewed with his new covenant. There was, however, no need for any speci-fically sacramental link concerning the eucharist and the covenant with Abraham, for that had its own direct link with the initiatory sacrament of baptism. To that we must now turn.

As we have already seen, to an insignificant nomadic Semite is held out a promise, timeless and limitless, that all the nations on earth will be blessed by and through his offspring. Abraham, sonless and married to an age-ing barren wife, believes the promise and the covenant is sealed by a sign—circumcision. All that follows in salvation history remains the outworking of that event.

Centuries pass and the child of the promise, Isaac, has become the ancestor of a growing nation which, freed from Egyptian slavery, gains national self-consciousness at Sinai by means of a related but separate covenant, and eventually develops into a geographically integrated people with its own homeland, ruled by a monarchy, focused on a temple ritual system, and challenged by a prophetic minority to fulfil its destiny as a holy nation with a world mission. In this way, the tensions between theologies of the kingdom, the priesthood, and the Suffering Servant hold uneasily together. Last in the old line, the prophet John challenges the nation to repentance and baptizes the penitent.

Jesus of Nazareth, as his followers believe, fulfilled the promised roles of anointed king, priest and lamb, and Suffering Servant. His new covenant, sealed by his blood on the cross, renders the old, Mosaic, covenant obsolete (Hebrews 8—10) but has no such effect on the covenant with Abraham, which, on the contrary, it endorses and fulfils (Romans 4 and Galatians 3—4). In short, the 'Old–New' contrast is between Sinai and Calvary, while the 'eternal covenant' with Abraham remains in force throughout the whole of salvation history.

The seal of the Abrahamic covenant is the 'outward and visible' sign of circumcision, a mark appropriate only to males (whether adult or infant). Paul, in writing to the Galatians, argues that those baptized into Christ, whether male or female, 'are Abraham's seed, heirs according to the promise' (Galatians 3:29). Thus circumcision is replaced by baptism (Colossians 2:11–12) as the sign and seal of the covenant by which God's promise and the respondent's faith are given a unique and objective character. Centuries later, when Martin Luther sought assurance for his wavering faith, it came from the affirmation *'baptizatus sum'* ('I have been baptized').

Consequential upon this understanding of the covenant, and of baptism as its sign and seal, the place of the infant children of believing parents is secured in a manner similar to that of Isaac, the child of the promise. But not only is the covenant inclusive of male heirs, as it is with the Jewish circumcision tradition; it is now inclusive of male and female infants. Paul, in his first letter to Corinth (7:14) speaks of the children of even one believing parent in a marriage as *hagia* (the holy covenant people), who are distinct from *akatharta* (the rest of humanity outside the covenant). It is the task of the former to bring the Good News to the latter.

It is within such an understanding of a covenant-making God's purposes for his people that baptism, whether of adult believers or of their infant children, seems to have been practised in the primitive and patristic Church. In the writings of Hippolytus, Origen and Augustine, the place of the infant of believing parents in the covenant community was signified by the act of baptism. In Hippolytus the practice is described, by Origen the continuity with the apostles is affirmed, and by Augustine the parallel with Abraham, Isaac and circumcision is indicated as part of its 'divine authority'.

A theology of the covenant is in no sense contrary to the other important facets of baptismal doctrine. Repentance from sin, identification with the cross, washing, incorporation into the Church, regeneration, death and resurrection, the renewal that comes from the Spirit, justification by grace—all these have their place within a full-orbed and rich theology of baptism.

The two sacraments of baptism and holy communion, says Tim Bradshaw, 'function as covenant "signs, seals, and pledges" of the work of God, focused narrowly upon the cross of Christ'. They are, he continues, 'vital for the church being ordained by the Lord himself. They stand in continuity with the Passover and the circumcision of ancient Israel'.[38]

Handley Moule summed this up well. He referred to both as being 'instances of the one idea—the giving of an external, and usually lasting or recurring, divine sign along with the divine promise'.[39] That's what a sacrament is—'an outward and visible sign of an inward and spiritual grace... ordained by Christ'.[40]

THE PROMISED LAND

We're almost there! I hope our tree symbol has been a help in getting the picture firmly implanted in our minds.

Remember, then, to look to Abraham. He holds the key to our understanding of the meaning of that amazing story of God's promise. Start there and you'll have a good chance of getting your doctrine of salvation—God's desire for all humanity—right. You won't make the all-too-common mistake of thinking that 'spirituality' is some totally private and individualistic search or experience. Instead you'll have begun to see that God has plans for a community, and the covenant is his promise to them. The Bible is, in short, the story of how that promise was given; how it developed into the themes of kingship, priesthood and prophecy; and reached its focus on a king, priest and Suffering Servant on a cross, who then sent his people out to the whole world—a royal, suffering servant, priestly community, whose horizons were the whole earth.

Finally, you will see the ultimate destiny of that redeemed community—the Church of Jesus, the Messiah. Through all this you may even discover why God has revealed himself as Trinity—three in one—Father, Son and the Holy Spirit.

Promises, promises. Signed, sealed and delivered. That's what God is all about. And, what's more, he keeps his promises.

A COVENANT HYMN

This is the truth which we proclaim,
God makes a promise firm and sure
marked by this sign made in his name,
here for our sickness God's own cure.

This is the grave in which we lie
dead to a world of sin and shame;
raised with our Lord, to self we die
and live to praise God's holy name.

This is the sacrament of birth
sealed by a saviour's death for sin.
Trust in his mercy all on earth,
open your hearts and let him in.

This is the covenant of grace,
God, to the nations, shows his love;
people of every tribe and race
born, by his Spirit, from above.

This is the badge we proudly wear,
washed by our God, the Three in One,
welcomed, in fellowship we share,
hope of eternal life begun.

© MICHAEL SAWARD

NOTES

1   J.I. Packer, 'Baptism: A Sacrament of the Covenant', *Churchman* 1955, p. 76.

2   R.C. Craston, *Baptism*, Bible Churchmen's Missionary Society, pp. 4, 7.

3   D. Van Biema, 'Abraham', *Time* Magazine, 30 September 2002.

4   G. Vermes, *Complete Dead Sea Scrolls in English*, Penguin, 1998, p. 67.

5   Packer, *Baptism*, pp. 79–80.

6   G.W. Bromiley, *Baptism and the Anglican Reformers*, Lutterworth, 1953, p. 101.

7   R. Brow, *Religion*, Tyndale, 1966, p. 20.

8   Brow, *Religion*, p. 27.

9   G. Byron, 'The Destruction of Sennacherib', 1815.

10 J.R.W. Stott, *Men with a Message*, Longmans, 1954, p. 6.

11 H.L. Ellison, *Men Spoke from God*, Paternoster, 1952, p. 13.

12 Ellison, *Men Spoke from God*, p. 44.

13 Ellison, *Men Spoke from God*, p. 44.

14 Ellison, *Men Spoke from God*, p. 55.

15 J. Skinner, cited in *The New Bible Dictionary*, IVF, 1962, p. 407.

16 A.B. Davidson, cited in J.B. Taylor, *Ezekiel*, Tyndale, 1969, p. 14.

17 J.B. Taylor, *Ezekiel*, Tyndale, 1969, p. 20.

18 J.A. Motyer, *The Prophecy of Isaiah*, IVP, 1993, p. 319.

19 C.R. North, *The Suffering Servant*, Oxford University Press, 1956, p. 142.

20 Motyer, *The Prophecy of Isaiah*, p. 320.

21 Motyer, *The Prophecy of Isaiah*, p. 386.

22 J. Goldingay, *God's Prophet: God's Servant*, Paternoster, 1984, p. 128.

23 Josephus, *Antiquities of the Jews* 14.4.4.

24 Josephus, *Antiquities of the Jews* 12.5.4.

25 Goldingay, *God's Prophet: God's Servant,* pp. 104–105.

26 W. Barclay, *John*, St Andrew Press, 1955, p. 301.

27 W. Barclay, *Matthew*, St Andrew Press, 1975, vol. 2, p. 371.

28 R.T. France, *Matthew*, IVP, 1985, p. 400.

29 W. Barclay, *Hebrews*, St Andrew Press, 1976, p. 5.

30 D. Guthrie, *Hebrews*, IVP, 1983, p. 32.

31 Martyrdom of Polycarp 3.2, *Early Christian Fathers,* ed. C.C Richardson, SCM, 1953, p. 150.

32 Josephus, *Antiquities of the Jews* 3.8.1.

33 W. Barclay, *Revelation*, St Andrew Press, 1976, p. 22.

34 D. Cohn-Sherbok, *The Crucified Jew*, Fount, 1992.

35 Consecration of a Bishop, *Alternative Service Book 1980*, SPCK, p. 387.

36 G. Bennett, *Crockford's Clerical Directory*, 1987.

37 J. Jewel, 'Apology', *Works* III. 100.

38 T. Bradshaw, *The Olive Branch*, Paternoster, 1992, p. 179.

39 H.E.C. Moule, *Outlines of Christian Doctrine*, Hodder, 1890, p. 239.

40 Book of Common Prayer 1662, Catechism.

Eight paragraphs on pages 109–112 were originally published as a part of Appendix A to *Christian Initiation*, Church House Publishing, 1991.

THE BIBLE AS A WHOLE

Stephen Travis

'What is the Bible? Not, as I once thought, a black book full of small print and obscure religious language. It is a whole collection of books which tell how God has made himself known to the human race and what is involved in responding to his love.'

In *The Bible as a Whole*, Stephen Travis presents the 'big picture' of how God's book fits together. With comment on 130 selected passages, it shows how the story of salvation unfolds from the beginnings of the Old Testament through to Revelation. Prayers and points for further thought offer ways of applyng the lessons learned to daily Christian living.

ISBN 1 84101 180 0   £9.99
To order, please turn to page 125.

THE SCEPTIC'S GUIDE TO READING THE BIBLE

A 'NO-STRINGS' EXPLORATION FOR THOSE WHO
HAVE GIVEN UP OR NEVER REALLY TRIED

Hilary Brand

Many people believe in God and respect the teachings of Jesus and yet find it almost impossible to read the Bible for themselves. It's too ancient; it's too difficult; it carries too much institutional baggage and, above all, it leaves more questions than answers. It's not surprising that apathy sets in!

This book aims to throw away the religious rulebook, scrape away preconceptions and offer a 'no strings' approach to reading the Bible. It suggests different approaches to the Bible's varied types of literature and offers a range of techniques for Bible reading, ranging from the imaginative to the analytical and from the broad sweep to the tiny phrase.

ISBN 1 84101 084 7   £7.99
To order, please turn to page 125.

FEASTING ON GOD'S WORD

FROM FROZEN FOOD TO GOURMET BANQUET

David Spriggs

The Bible is a neglected treasure—one that we ignore at our peril—yet fewer and fewer people read it these days, not only in wider society but even in the Christian community. This book is written to reverse that trend, to motivate Christians of all ages to experience the power of the Bible in new ways.

Packed with imaginative suggestions for enjoying the Bible, from 'Eat it' to 'Display it' to 'Twist it', this is a book that will help us turn the 'frozen food' of scripture into a gourmet banquet, at which we can sit down to feast on God.

ISBN 1 84101 222 X   £6.99
To order, please turn to page 125.

FROM ORPHANS TO HEIRS

CELEBRATING OUR SPIRITUAL ADOPTION

Mark Stibbe

The key to our liberation as Christians is the biblical image of spiritual adoption. So often we continue to live as spiritual orphans, forgetting that thanks to the saving work of Jesus we have been made sons and daughters of God.

From Orphans to Heirs explores this image of adoption, much neglected as a way of understanding our salvation, yet crucial in an age when so many people are searching for intimacy. Mark Stibbe also shares his own story of growing up as an adopted child and the insights his experiences gave him into the heart of God, our adopting Father.

ISBN 1 84101 023 5   £6.99
To order, please turn to page 125.

ORDER FORM

REF	TITLE	PRICE	QTY	TOTAL
180 0	*The Bible as a Whole*	£9.99		
084 7	*The Sceptic's Guide to Reading the Bible*	£7.99		
222 X	*Feasting on God's Word*	£6.99		
023 5	*From Orphans to Heirs*	£6.99		

POSTAGE AND PACKING CHARGES					
order value	UK	Europe	Surface	Air Mail	
£7.00 & under	£1.25	£3.00	£3.50	£5.50	
£7.01–£30.00	£2.25	£5.50	£6.50	£10.00	
Over £30.00	free	prices on request			

Postage/packing:

Donation:

Total enclosed:

Name _____ Account no _____

Address _____

_____ Postcode _____

Tel. _____ Email _____

Total enclosed £ _____ (cheques made payable to 'BRF')

Payment by: cheque ❑ postal order ❑ Visa ❑

Mastercard ❑ Switch ❑

Card no: ☐☐☐☐☐☐☐☐☐☐☐☐☐☐☐☐☐☐

Expiry date of card: ☐☐☐☐   Issue no (Switch): | | | | |

Signature (essential if paying by credit/Switch card) _____

All orders must be accompanied by the appropriate payment.

Please send your completed order form to:
BRF, First Floor, Elsfield Hall, 15–17 Elsfield Way, Oxford OX2 8FG
Tel 01865 319700 / Fax 01865 319701
Email: enquiries@brf.org.uk

❑ Please send me further information about BRF publications.

Available from your local Christian bookshop.   BRF is a Registered Charity